POWER AND PASSION

RAY McCAULEY
WITH
RON STEELE

POWER AND
PASSION

*Fulfilling God's Destiny
for the Nation*

STRUIK CHRISTIAN BOOKS

Authors' note: Except for the sermons which have been adapted, comments in all other chapters are those of Ron Steele.

Struik Christian Books Ltd
(A member of the Struik Publishing Group (Pty) Ltd)
Cornelis Struik House
80 McKenzie Street
Cape Town 8001

Reg. No. 04/02203/06

This edition 1996

First published 1996

Edited by Hilda Hermann
DTP by Rhonda Crouse
Cover design by Odette Marais
Cover reproduction by Positive Image cc, Cape Town
Reproduction by Cape Imaging Bureau, Woodstock
Printed and bound by CTP Book Printers (Pty) Ltd,
PO Box 6060, Parow East 7501

ISBN 1 86823 282 4

CONTENTS

Prologue

The dusky silhouette of the Hercules cargo plane sat like a brooding dinosaur at Waterkloof military base in Pretoria. As slivers of sunlight began to touch the clouds, a line of men and women shuffled through the gate and boarded the aircraft.

They were a most remarkably ragtag group. There were international television reporters, South African government officials, a Deputy Minister of Foreign Affairs, and a band of religious people that included Muslims, Jews and Christians.

Scrambling into the cavernous body of the Hercules, these people were confronted by a storehouse of goods bearing white stickers which read: 'To Rwanda: with love from Operation Mercy.'

Suddenly the mighty engines of the plane roared. The chatter ceased as the deafening noise of the engines shook and vibrated through the plane as it trundled along the runway. Moments later the aircraft was cleared for take-off. Then, like a clumsy albatross, the Hercules roared down the concrete strip and began to lift into the crisp air of a frosty highveld winter's morning.

Five hours later the passengers would land in sweltering tropical heat at the Tanzanian town of Mwanza on Lake Victoria. From there, some would fly to the tiny village of Ngara, which almost overnight had become one of the largest refugee camps in Africa.

The tons of food and medical supplies had to be transported from Mwanza along a tortuous strip of road to the refugee camp. Hundreds of desperate refugees were fleeing daily from the bloody death and destruction of ethnic hatred that gripped the lush, landlocked nation of Rwanda.

The Hercules aircraft and the journalists, government officials and religious people made history for South Africa, which only 11 weeks earlier had been transformed from a White-dominated government to a democracy that saw power transferred to the majority black population.

This mercy flight of food, medical supplies and clothing was a first for the new democratic South Africa. The gesture firmly identified the nation with the rest of Africa.

More significantly, though, was the fact that this mercy mission had been initiated by the church in South Africa. Probably the most remarkable aspect of the whole project was the fact that the prime mover was Pentecostal minister, Ray McCauley. The task of coordinating and making Operation Mercy a national project rested with Ray after his local church initiated a low-key appeal for goods for the starving Rwandan refugees.

This sort of initiative was exceptional for the simple fact that the main force behind the mercy mission was a local church and that ministers like Ray were often sidelined from national affairs. In South Africa, the Pentecostal churches, the roots of the Rhema congregation, were often scorned by the previous government during the apartheid era.

During the years of apartheid, the Pentecostal churches received few favours from the government. Instead, the Dutch Reformed Church, which was aligned with the government of the day, received special treatment, especially when it came to radio and television airtime.

The other side of the coin is that Pentecostals, traditionally, shunned political involvement. Their typically pietistic approach made them zealous to win the lost, but few ventured into the world of politics and social injustices.

As a result, few Pentecostal leaders in South Africa, especially among the white denominations, ever uttered a whimper of protest against the human indignities that apartheid imposed upon millions of people. It was easier to ignore the contradiction of Scripture and pacify their conscience by offering a prayer.

Therefore, during the 40-odd year struggle to rid South Africa of its racist government, very few Pentecostal leaders won any stripes for speaking out in opposition. It was left to the men of the cloth in the historical churches, like Father Trevor Huddlestone, Reverend Beyers Naude – an Afrikaner who was treated as a traitor by his own people, and later

Archbishop Desmond Tutu, to bear the banners that cried for justice and equity.

Of course, these outspoken critics of apartheid were heavily branded as enemies of the State and an impressive government propaganda machine labelled these clerics as communists. In fact, any form of protest against apartheid, whether it came from the liberal English-speaking press or from open-minded university students, was easily tarnished with the red brush of communism. This not so subtle form of brainwashing worked brilliantly to neutralise the majority of Pentecostal believers in South Africa.

The communist bogey man, portrayed as a direct threat to Christianity and religious freedom, played right into the Pentecostal preoccupation with end-time events which, in those days, saw the Red Bear as the nation most likely to fulfil the book of Revelation.

As a result, the Pentecostal churches and their leaders hardly ever touched the murky waters of politics or simple human justice. They believed their calling was high above such matters. The outcome was that the Pentecostals were seen as supporters of apartheid.

There were a few Pentecostals, black and white, who did raise their lonely voices, but they were merely seen as people who had succumbed to liberal or communist brainwashing.

From the Nationalist government's point of view this allowed them greater freedom to harass and persecute the likes of Beyers Naude, Dr Frank Chikane, former secretary of the South African Council of Churches, Archbishop Desmond Tutu and many others. It also meant that many of the historical church leaders took a very negative view of the spineless behaviour of the Christianity espoused by the Pentecostals. Those involved with the struggle, like the then banned African National Congress (ANC) and the Pan Africanist Congress (PAC), had little time for the Pentecostals. They did not trust them and saw them as props for the apartheid regime and regarded them as racist.

It is from this arguably dubious background that Ray McCauley and the Rhema Church in South Africa arose.

It is out of this stained part of Pentecostal church history that Ray has emerged with his congregation as a challenge to Christian leaders to make the difference – not only in their communities, but also in their nations.

The Rhema Church is setting new limits and goals for other churches and leaders to follow. In fact, its programme of evangelism, linked with a strong social programme, is making a splendid statement in South Africa. Its influence and that of Ray and his wonderful team of pastors and staff, places them in a position that few evangelical churches or ministers have enjoyed in the country.

Of course, it has not come easily. It has been difficult to shrug off the clinging webs of apathy and suspicion. This has meant challenging the stereotype of Pentecostal Christianity. It has meant transforming one's thinking and seeing the role of the church in a much broader and grander scope.

The aim and the direction of this book are to inspire and challenge Christian leaders and their churches in all parts of the world. The trail-blazing of Ray and his congregation is producing fruit that should rouse the spirits of leaders to realise that God can do extraordinary things through His people and His church.

The purpose of this book is not only to exhort leaders to accept the role that the church can play in the existence of a nation, but to give practical examples of how it is possible to influence a nation for God.

For the purposes of this book, the role of the church is divided into four basic components:

❑ The prophetic relevance of the church in a nation;
❑ The social significance of the church in a nation;
❑ The evangelistic potency of the church in a nation; and
❑ The refreshing of the church for its continuing task.

Besides the biblical teachings on each of these divisions, illustrations of how the Rhema Church has progressed in South Africa during the past seven years will provide practical pointers on what it means for a leader to take his church into the battlefield of life issues. For too long, the church has been playing in the playground's sandpit. The challenge of the hour is to make the gospel relevant, significant and potent in today's real world.

PART ONE
PROPHETICALLY RELEVANT

1 THE JOSEPH FACTOR

Adapted from a sermon by Ray McCauley

In Haggai 1:7–9 we read:

> 'Thus says the Lord of hosts: "Consider your ways!
> Go up to the mountains and bring wood and build the
> temple, that I may take pleasure in it and be glorified,"
> says the Lord. "You looked for much, but indeed it
> came to little; and when you brought it home, I blew
> it away. Why?" says the Lord of hosts. "Because of
> My house that is in ruins, while every one of you runs
> to his own house."'

One important thing learnt in Rhema's experience over the
years is that God requires unity, not exclusively on doctrine,
but rather unity of spirit.

It is important to agree on the basic foundations of the
gospel, but it is becoming more obvious that God wants the
church to achieve a new unity, not only in South Africa, but
around the world. This cannot happen on the basis of doctrine because there are shades of emphasis among church
groups. However, I believe that God is demanding a unity of
spirit and purpose from Christians around the world.

Unfortunately, many Christians and even ministers are running around doing their own thing and hardly give the time of
day to anyone else. They find it difficult to work with others.
Haggai 2:3–8 reads:

> '"Who is left among you who saw this temple in its
> former glory? And how do you see it now? In compar-
> ison with it, is this not in your eyes as nothing? Yet
> now be strong Zerubbabel," says the Lord; "and be
> strong, Joshua, son of Jehozadak, the high priest; and
> be strong, all you people of the land," says the Lord,

"and work; for I am with you," says the Lord of hosts.
"According to the word that I covenanted with you
when you came out of Egypt, so My Spirit remains
among you; do not fear!" For thus says the Lord of
hosts: "Once more (it is a little while) I will shake
heaven and earth, the sea and dry land; and I will shake
all nations, and they shall come to the Desire of All
Nations, and I will fill this temple with glory," says the
Lord of hosts. "The silver is Mine, and the gold is
Mine," says the Lord of hosts.'

For the church to play its rightful role in the world, one point
needs to be settled at the outset: it's going to take money to
achieve the objective that God wants for His people.

Haggai 2:9 continues:

"'The glory of this latter temple shall be greater than
the former," says the Lord of hosts. "And in this place
I will give peace," says the Lord of hosts.'

These verses have been the inspiration for what I believe is
the role of the church today. They have inspired me to become even more determined that the church should achieve
its destiny in South Africa and in other nations of the world.
Visions and dreams, though, sometimes collide with obstacles when we try to fulfil them.

In the Old Testament there is the inspiring story of Joseph,
the dreamer. Although this story is well known, it is possible
that Christian leaders may have missed some of the more
salient points about the prophetic influence that Joseph had,
not only on the Egyptians, but on his own people.

It was the prophetic insight into Pharaoh's dream – and
remember, God gave the dream to an unbeliever – that opened
the doors of blessing for so many people. It was Joseph who
brought the interpretation that ministered to Pharaoh and
caused an entire nation to be fed and preserved.

Joseph's prophetic influence also caused the Egyptians to
look to Joseph as a man of God.

Sadly, over the years, the church has fallen short in its definition, understanding and administration of the prophetic voice and gifts.

To be blunt, most churches in the Pentecostal/charismatic traditions have only dealt with a very shallow part of the prophetic voice and potential influence of the church. They have missed many wonderful opportunities to be heard in the affairs of the nation.

Most of what happens in many Pentecostal services is just a babbling, 'Yeah, ye and yeah, ye and the Lord says we're all good, and the Lord loves you all, and God gives, and God blesses,' and so on.

Now, this is not always wrong, but they are usually words of encouragement or exhortations for the congregation. They do not really have any influence beyond the local church. What is lacking is the strong and forthright, 'Thus says the Lord,' and in steps the man of God to confront the broader issues of the day.

The church needs to look to prophetically influencing and changing the heart of the nation.

I believe the voice of God will soon be heard in greater volume around the world, to challenge the decline of morals and to give direction in matters of crime and violence, which plague not only South Africa but stalk many other nations.

Rather than follow the politicians, the church must lead them. The church must proclaim God's standards prophetically. The bold, prophetic word must go out to the nations.

There is a warning, though. There are many voices in the wind and unless the church stands up and proclaims by the anointing of God and, with the support and unity of God's people, the witness will be muted. That is why the message of this book is deemed so important and relevant to the church today. There are many enticing voices ringing through the corridors and the church needs to know the voice of the true Shepherd.

To achieve this exciting destiny and to have a greater influence in our nations is going to demand greater commitment, greater giving financially and greater sacrifices.

Look again at the life of Joseph as it is recorded in Genesis and at how the prophetic ministry operated in his life. In fact, it was not very glamorous. When he had his first prophetic dream, he was thrown into a pit and almost lost his life. However, God had a plan and purpose for Joseph's life that was linked to the lives of millions of people.

It is a staggering thought to consider that the wellbeing of other people hung on a thread when Joseph was tossed into the pit. Yet, over the events was the hand of God. What looked like a dead-end for the young dreamer was, in reality, the beginning of a road to greatness. It was not going to be an easy road, but God's destiny for Joseph, the nation of Israel and the Egyptians could not be thwarted.

A strange anomaly among Pentecostals and charismatics is their total disregard for the consistency of Scripture when it comes to hearing and receiving a prophetic word. The word is explicit in John 16:13 when it says that '... when He, the Spirit of truth, has come, He will guide you into all truth'. Yet few, it seems, are able to know or hear the voice of the Holy Spirit.

Many white South Africans were in a state of confusion and even abject fear during the run-up to the democratic elections of April 1994. Unfortunately, many of them were Christians and, sadly, there were many Pentecostals among them. At that time, the country was rife with rumours and so-called prophecies.

Most of them were complete nonsense. So-called prophets sounded off in Pentecostal churches across the country stamped, of course, with the divine seal of, 'thus saith the Lord'. There were even claims that the Lord Jesus Christ had appeared and given one saint the earth-shattering commission to call the country to prayer!

This may have sounded very noble and many believed that it truly was a divine visitation. Many thousands did pray. However, tens of thousands of Christians of all denominations had been praying for many, many months. Paul's exhortation to 'pray without ceasing' surely did not need such dramatic reinforcement?

The time before South Africa's first-ever democratic general election was undeniably a period of great uncertainty for everyone. It was certainly the time for a clear voice to speak in the name of God. But the problem was that only a few were listening to the men who wear that awesome credential with respect and dignity.

Lamentably, thousands of Christians ran to hear the voice of the false prophets. The reason? They wanted their ears tickled with the things they wanted to hear. The pronouncements being made satisfied inner racist fears and prejudices.

Despite this clamour, I consistently proclaimed that the election would be a success and that God would see the nation through. There were moments of doubt, but as I examined the facts and the way in which God had been leading us over the years, I had to conclude that He would not let the nation end in a bloodbath.

That, of course, was what many whites believed, including many Christians. Many thought a civil war was just around the corner. Blacks on the other hand, including the majority of black Christians, hailed the forthcoming elections as the greatest event in the nation's history and, of course, the end of white domination.

The reason for some white apprehension was not difficult to understand, especially for those who had treated blacks with little respect. The depressing fact, however, was the behaviour of so many Pentecostal Christians who, as Bible-believers, should have known better.

One self-styled prophet from England brought a word from the Lord at a church in Durban. In essence, the prophecy was doom and gloom, with blood flowing in the streets.

A well-known conservative Christian newsletter published a special edition warning the church of the impending demise of religious freedom. It predicted shortages of food and medical supplies, and even gave Christians a shopping list of essential items. Instead of the church taking the lead, it joined the rabble in the shopping malls fighting over tinned foods! There were many Christians who felt the urge either to emigrate or to take an overseas holiday during election time, just in case the revolution started. It was laughable and illustrated the lack of the church's prophetic role, or at least its inability to discern the voice of a true prophet.

Even within our own congregation, and among many fellow ministers, there was a negative attitude towards the elections and a fear that the worst would happen. It seems that when people give in to that sort of attitude, they find it much easier to receive a bad report. But God gave me a strong inner witness that everything would be all right.

April 27, 1994 was an amazingly peaceful day in which millions of blacks and whites queued side by side for up to eights hours to cast their votes. There was no violence, no shortage of fuel, food or anything else. In reality, there was only an oversupply of love and joy. God was smiling gracefully upon South Africa.

Although we may criticise the Christians in South Africa, a similar charge can be laid against the church worldwide for its impotence in foretelling years in advance that the Berlin Wall would come down.

Also, why didn't the church proclaim ten years ago the dissolution of the mighty Soviet Empire and the decline of communism? Instead, we had the 'Yeah ye' chorus of the 'Russians are coming'! Books were churned out by the dozen but none, to my knowledge, ever predicted what really happened. They simply made their writers rich and confused millions of Christians.

There is no doubt that God can show us things to come, what is needed and what He wants from His people. It is a matter of hearing and discerning the truth. It is also a matter of establishing credibility through integrity. That is seen in the life of Joseph.

While he was in prison, Joseph interpreted the butler's dream. Although forgotten for a while, it was the beginning because it established Joseph's credibility and reputation.

Jesus gave plain guidance when he said that you can judge people by their fruit. Even an unbeliever has enough sense to look at a person's track record when it comes to influencing his own life. Even an unbeliever will be wary before entering a business partnership. They will thoroughly check whether that person is credit worthy, and what sort of business record and background they have.

This seems to be an area where Christian leaders often fail. The fruit needs to be checked. The credibility needs to be above reproach. The integrity needs to be of the purest.

Another pivotal point in Joseph's life was when Pharaoh called for him to interpret his troublesome dream.

The first thing that amazes us is that God gave an unbeliever this dream. This man was not the head of a church, he was no apostle, he was no prophet, and he was no spiritual giant. In fact, he was a pagan.

It is obvious God had a plan for this man's life. That is something we need to recognise and watch out for. God does not work exclusively within the Pentecostal church. God sometimes uses a rank unbeliever or a person from one of those 'other' churches.

One of the most outstanding modern examples of a man whom God has used is South Africa's President, Nelson Mandela. He endured 27 years of imprisonment and came out with no bitterness or thought of revenge. Instead, he has been the model of compromise and appeasement to militant whites, although some still distrust him and his political party. His achievements and his diplomacy mark him as a great man and undoubtedly a man of destiny in God's greater universal plan.

If a modern-day pharaoh called for a man of God today, one wonders how many would respond, especially if he was a heathen. Fortunately, Joseph was a man of faith and action. He knew his prophetic calling and was not afraid to confront Pharaoh with the truth. There was no fear of compromise.

It is the church and its leaders who will influence the current political and business community. They are the ones who can bring change and direction that will lead nations in a godly way.

Joseph's prophetic ministry, though, was not always a happy one. He endured temptation, false accusations, neglect and persecution, yet he never lost his faith in God. Somehow he knew that he was not born to be a slave, but a ruler. From the beginning he was a man of purpose and leadership; nothing could stop him from fulfilling his destiny.

It is a tough fact of our Christian experience that we sometimes have to endure resistance. Most times it shapes us into better people. And even in times of resistance, God will take what the devil brings against you, and turn it around for your benefit. Romans 8:28 states:

> 'And we know that all things work together for good to those who love God, to those who are the called according to His purpose.'

That was certainly true in Joseph's life. From the forgotten dungeon he became the prime minister, so to speak. The story of Joseph clearly displays God's concern for even an unbelieving nation. How much more concerned is God today for the nations of the world?

What is needed are more men of whom it can be said, as in Genesis 41:38:

> 'Can we find such a one as this, a man in whom is the Spirit of God?'

Joseph was full of God. He wasn't lukewarm, he wasn't a compromiser, he wasn't someone who turned his back on God. He was a man who stood out in the crowd; he was always the salt and the light. He was prophetically relevant to his generation and to future generations.

2   In the Crossfire

Possibly the reason why many church leaders back off or become timid when it comes to tampering with the affairs of a nation is the price that has to be paid.

Some of our critics perceive that Ray McCauley is just glory-hunting, in search of television and newspaper headlines. Few understand the frustration, pressure and mental energy that goes with the involvement.

Often one is misunderstood, not only by close associates, but by the very politicians one tries to help and influence.

True to human nature, politicians seem overkeen to cry out for spiritual help when they are in a cul de sac, but once they have a quick solution, God and the church often get brushed into a dusty corner of their public lives.

Despite these frustrations, Ray has ventured deeper and deeper into the murky waters of political power play. Initially they were small tippy-toe ventures in the shallow end, but when South Africa found itself catapulted into a social and political transformation in the 1990s, he plunged into the deep end.

Interestingly, some political leaders with whom Ray had dealings over the past seven or eight years are no longer in office. Dr Andries Treurnicht, one-time leader of the Conservative Party, has passed away; Lucas Mangope of Bophuthatswana was deposed; and Brigadier Oupa Gqozo of Ciskei was forced out of office.

In his meetings with these men and other national leaders, including President Nelson Mandela, Mr FW de Klerk and Chief Mangosuthu Buthelezi, Ray has repeatedly urged the need for Godly justice, peace and reconciliation. Regrettably, his wise counsel has often been ignored or evaded.

The case of Brigadier Oupa Gqozo is a classic example. The diminutive Brigadier and some of his fellow officers attended the Rhema Church occasionally and got to know Ray. It appeared to be a God-given opportunity to contribute to the life of a leader, albeit a minor one in the greater context of South Africa.

As the build up to the democratic process gathered momentum in 1992, the Brigadier, who was regarded by the dominant ANC political party as a stooge for the South African government, came under increasing pressure and hostility from the ANC and other political groupings in his home territory of the Ciskei.

One night he telephoned Ray, and requested an urgent meeting the following morning.

I was at Ray's house that morning when a small convoy of vehicles transporting bodyguards, aides and Brigadier Gqozo swirled round the driveway.

The Brigadier told Ray about the crisis facing him in the Ciskei. The Brigadier claimed that the ANC was attempting to overthrow him and that a mass march was being planned.

Ray asked pertinently whether the Brigadier believed that God had allowed him to become the ruler of Ciskei. The Brigadier affirmed that he believed this. Ray challenged him to call a referendum and allow the voices of the people to be heard. 'If God placed you in power, then surely you must trust him to keep you there,' argued Ray.

The Brigadier half-heartedly agreed, but said that a referendum was not feasible because the ANC would intimidate the people. Ray countered this by offering to involve impartial observers to ensure a free and just process.

Brigadier Gqozo thanked Ray for his advice, but when asked what he was going to do about the threatened mass action in Bisho, he retorted: 'Don't worry about it. I'll take care of it on Monday.'

Just 48 hours later, on Monday, 7 September 1992, the Bisho Massacre occurred. A large group of ANC demonstrators marched to the government offices of Brigadier Gqozo and, as they neared their objective, 28 people were cut down by a merciless volley of gunfire from Ciskei troops.

Later that same night, Brigadier Gqozo called Ray, begging him to meet him the next morning and advise him on an incident that made news headlines around the world.

In response to this plea, Ray and I flew to East London and spent the day with the Brigadier, some of his chief advisers and a deputation of local church ministers. It was an exhausting and at times nerve-wracking day.

Ray spent the first two hours alternating between private meetings with the Brigadier and the Ciskei Council members. A local church delegation arrived and there was more parleying, but neither the Brigadier or his advisers would budge on their position that their action had been correct. They regretted the loss of life, but blamed 'Red Ronnie' Kasrils, a member of the ANC who had been prominent in the previous day's tragic march. Kasrils later became Deputy Minister of Defence in the Government of National Unity.

Nobel Peace Prize winner, Archbishop Desmond Tutu, also arrived in an effort to stave off more bloodshed.

The tension in the area was palpable and the smell of death seemed to linger in the air. Piercing eyes stared at us and, sure enough, hidden behind trees or in a depression in the ground one caught sight of a soldier with a strategically pointed rifle.

A large militant group of ANC supporters, many of whom had lost loved ones and family members in the previous day's shooting, had gathered on a dusty road near the civic buildings. We asked our driver to take us to this group because we believed Archbishop Tutu was there. However, he declined to take us all the way, fearing the crowd would turn hostile when they recognised him as one of the Brigadier's men.

We had to make our way to the mob on foot, with apprehension. As we walked the sandy road with determined strides, I wondered what would happen if the crowd turned against us.

As Ray and I drew near, some men walked towards us and greeted us with shouts of 'Amandla!' and a clench-fisted salute. This was a shout of liberation and we both responded with charismatic waves and a 'Hallelujah!', peppered with a muffled 'Amandla!' or two.

Mentioning Archbishop Tutu's name brought smiles to their faces and when we explained that we, too, were ministers of the gospel, we were greeted warmly.

Later we met with Archbishop Tutu and other clergy at a nearby hotel, where we tried to piece together a media statement and discuss ways of defusing what was still a highly volatile situation.

Ray, who had spent more time than anyone else that day with the Brigadier, issued a media statement that reflected the day's events:

'I believe that Brigadier Gqozo is committed to seeking a democratic mandate from the people of Ciskei.

'I have spent hours with him in private sessions and although he has publicly said that he will not call a referendum now, I believe that he will do so when he believes the time is right.

'I flew to Bisho to try to persuade him to give a positive signal to defuse the tension and to make sure he met with Archbishop Tutu and Dr Frank Chikane, of the South African Council of Churches.

'Brigadier Gqozo has told me that, as a God-fearing Christian, he believes in allowing his public support to be tested by a true democratic process.

'However, my impression is that he does not want to be steamrollered into something at this time, but is hoping that once calm has returned, he will announce a referendum.

'The decision, though, will be his own, but I have advised him that as a Christian he needs to allow a democratic process to take place.

'There are problems concerning fear and intimidation, but I believe that if the Brigadier can be assured that there will be impartial monitors for any future referendum, then he will go to the people for a mandate.

'He has also told me that if the people reject him, which he says is unlikely, then he will accept that decision.'

An army helicopter took us to East London's airport, where a commercial flight had been delayed for us. Ray then candidly admitted that he felt the Brigadier's political career would end within the next few weeks.

Amazingly, the Brigadier managed to retain office for another 18 months, during which time he openly attacked Ray and accused him of giving him poor advice. He accused him of taking sides with the ANC.

Just weeks before Brigadier Gqozo stepped down and handed over the reins of his administration to a transitional authority, his wife telephoned Ray and admitted that her husband had been wrong in not accepting the advice given to him 18 months previously.

This is just one of many cameo roles Ray played during the years of negotiation for a non-racial democracy. But none was as difficult or as complex as his dealings with the Zulu leader Chief Mangosuthu Buthelezi and King Goodwill Zwelithini, the official monarch of the Zulu people.

During the critical negotiation period, which was threatened by right-wing extremists, militant Zulus and left-wing elements, Ray repeatedly appealed for the major leaders to get together, with the church as the referee.

Prior to the April 1994 election, the country experienced intense violence. Although not nationwide, the brutality experienced in KwaZulu-Natal was particularly bad.

Although there were sporadic incidents of violence in other areas, notably the greater Johannesburg area, it was the Zulu nation that was seen to hold the key to a peaceful and meaningful election.

Throughout this difficult and often heartbreaking period, church leaders repeatedly tried to intervene to restore peace and bring reconciliation. Sadly, many attempts to curb the violence did not bear fruit, mainly because of the stubbornness of the major political leaders.

The country was close to turmoil, right-wing groups threatening a scorched-earth policy. Most doubted their ability or resolve to carry out such extreme tactics, but the propaganda fuelled white fears that the blacks would seek to avenge the years of deprivation under apartheid rule.

In KwaZulu-Natal the Inkatha Freedom Party (IFP) was

involved in a deadly confrontation with ANC supporters. Neither the IFP nor the ANC had clean hands in an area of the country that threatened to become an African Bosnia.

There was also the perception that relationships between the major leaders – Mandela, De Klerk and Buthelezi – were deteriorating. This threatened to delay the democratic process and Ray launched a major initiative to get the 'Big Three' together in a prayer service. We thought that a prayer service would be the most neutral setting and that seeing the three leaders together would help to calm the masses.

The idea grew and other important leaders were included. A venue was selected and when Ray flew to Cape Town to personally invite President de Klerk, it appeared that the impossible could happen. There was an added boost when American President Bill Clinton heard of the initiative and some tentative plans were made to enable him to participate in a special satellite link-up with the proposed prayer service.

After getting President de Klerk to agree to attend, Ray returned to Johannesburg and announced to the media that all the major political players had agreed, in principle, to the united prayer service. Then he experienced the fickleness of professional politicians who drag their feet. There was also a hint that Ray should not be the one to bring off such a coup and all the hard work, negotiations and time went down the drain.

Several months later, the Methodist Bishop Stanley Magoba, Chairman of the National Peace Committee, Archbishop Tutu, and other churchmen eventually succeeded in getting Mandela and Buthelezi together for a private meeting.

However, as noble as that effort was, it was not enough to heal a widening rift that began to scream a red alert to the nation. Despite all the negotiations and all the talking and exchange of ideas around the table, the country looked doomed for a major civil war.

When the fireworks, car hooters and singing which heralded in 1994 had disappeared, South Africans of all races contemplated the new year with mixed feelings. For whites, the feeling was mainly fear or, at best, resignation to more violence and trouble. For blacks there was the expectation of voting for the first time in their lives. This simple democratic right buoyed the black population despite their doubts for the future. There was an unbridled expectancy that political freedom was within reach.

Serious-minded people of all races had to admit that the level of violence and destruction was endangering the April elections. A sense of hopelessness and resignation to dangerous and possibly nationwide conflict began to creep into the thoughts of many people. Against this background, Ray enthusiastically accepted an invitation to speak at a special conference promoted as 'Vision '94'. It was coordinated by the South African Council of Churches and was attended by most of the country's leading churchmen.

During the conference, Ray was once again moved to set in motion another attempt to draw together the major political leaders. He hoped that with the support of the South African Council of Churches a leaders' summit would succeed.

In making his plea for intervention, Ray said:

'Nobody seems able to offer a solution and we need God to help us in this time of national crisis.

'I believe the church can and must offer to intervene. Together we represent about half of the country's population. It is the church that has to bury people, care for the orphans and widows, and deal with all the human trauma caused by the violence.

'It is time that we call all political leaders to account to the ordinary people in the street and make them realise that thousands of innocent lives are at stake.

'I do not offer a political solution, but rather the moral force of the church to challenge the conscience of political leaders to stop their war-talk, and to get together and find lasting solutions. One of my suggestions is that we call a summit meeting of political leaders that will be facilitated and mediated by the church.'

This effort was endorsed by the most prominent church leaders in the country, but the summit failed to materialise and sadly, it looked like the threads of peace were tearing apart.

Despite the collapse of yet another peace initiative, Ray continued to keep an eye on the situation, looking for an opportunity to offer the church's assistance. Other church leaders, particularly those in KwaZulu-Natal like Michael Cassidy of Africa Enterprise, an evangelistic organisation, and Bishop Khosa Mgojo, a Methodist and president of the South African Council of Churches – did not give up. The behind-the-scenes activity continued.

Sadly, the perception filtered through that some political players were not keen for the church to be involved in all this shuttle diplomacy. This became obvious when the politicians looked to the former American Secretary of State, Henry Kissinger, and Britain's former representative at the United Nations, Lord Carrington, as international mediators.

However, while efforts were being made by the politicians, Ray persuaded the chairman of the National Peace Committee, John Hall, that he and a group of churchmen, including Archbishop Tutu, should go to the king of the Zulus.

This they did on 15 April, only 12 days before the 27 April general election. They spent six hours with the king, with Ray and Archbishop Tutu ministering and encouraging the king to rise above party politics. As a result the king made a strong, nationwide call to all Zulus to stop fighting. This influential visit made a vital contribution to major decisions that were to follow within the next few days.

At the same time, a Kenyan economist, Professor Washington Okumu, who had been persuaded by Michael Cassidy to join the international mediation team, stayed on after the other mediators left. Kissinger and Lord Carrington left South Africa convinced that there was no hope of bringing Buthelezi into the April election. They left despondent and with little hope of averting a civil war. However, the divine hand of God continued to direct the course of the nation, thanks to the fervent prayers of tens of thousands of Christians and the tireless efforts of many churchmen.

Professor Okumu, as it turned out, proved to be the Lord's wildcard in the unfolding drama of the nation. He drew up a document which was shuttled among the principal leaders.

Significantly, a large Jesus Peace Rally, organised by KwaZulu-Natal church leaders, took place in Durban on 17 April. Nearly 30 000 Christians gathered to pray for an improvement in the political situation of the nation.

Unknown to most, Professor Okumu was having a private meeting with Buthelezi, the KwaZulu-Natal ANC leader, Jacob Zuma and the then Home Affairs Minister, Danie Schutte.

It was during the time of the prayer rally that these leaders created a compromise document that was taken to De Klerk and Mandela. Some 48 hours later Buthelezi announced that his party would take part in the elections. A potential national calamity had been prevented and the church could rightly rejoice in the fact that God's hand had clearly been visible in this amazing turnabout.

Besides the efforts of the Christian leaders, millions of Christians in South Africa, the United States, Australia and Europe had been alerted by various Christian networks, proving beyond doubt that God answers fervent prayers.

It was gratifying to hear Buthelezi publicly acknowledge God's intervention in bringing him and his political party into the election process.

The following are extracts from Buthelezi's speech, which was broadcast live to the nation on 19 April 1994, just eight days before the general election:

'The Inkatha Freedom Party has decided to make the kind of compromises which will make its entry into the election possible in order to avoid a great deal more bloodshed and carnage the likes of which we have witnessed in recent months ... I wish to convey my deep gratitude to Professor Washington Ukumu for the role he played in making it possible to reach the agreement that will result in the IFP entering the election.

'He was an additional appointment as advisor to the international mediating team and remained on in South Africa when the other mediators left. It was his personal intervention that made the final negotiation breakthrough possible.

'When my spirits were down after the international mediation had been aborted and I was leaving Johannesburg for Ulundi on 15 April, I received a message at the airport from Professor Okumu that he wanted to meet me and would be there in 20 minutes.

'I have known Professor Okumu for more than 20 years, having met him at a prayer breakfast in Washington, and we have kept in touch on the basis of Christian fellowship.

'I waited at Lanseria airport for as long as I could on the morning of 15 April for Professor Okumu but as two of my colleagues had an appointment with His Majesty the King I had to leave.

'However, the aircraft had been airborne for only a few minutes when I was told there was a problem and we had to turn back.

'Fortunately Prof Okumu was there and I said that it was as though God had prevented me from leaving; I was like Jonah brought back. I told Professor Okumu that my forced return was a godsend ...'

Professor Okumu, in a brief speech at the same international media conference, was not ashamed to give the glory to God, and at one stage made the remark:

'Jesus Christ shed His blood for South Africa and we do not need to spill any more ...'

The hand of God was gently shepherding South Africa on its new road to justice, reconciliation and true peace.

3 PAYING THE PRICE

The political hierarchy can be very touchy about church ministers meddling in its affairs and this was the case when South Africans awoke on a bitter winter's morning in June 1992 to hear of yet another appalling massacre. It took place in a black township called Boipatong, situated about 70 km south of Johannesburg, near the industrial areas of Vereeniging and Vanderbijlpark. During the night a group of armed men had raided the rudimentary tin shacks and embarked on a killing spree. They had swept through the houses, shooting and beating people indiscriminately. In a matter of minutes the air was filled with cries of death and destruction and the attack ended as suddenly as it had begun.

Ray McCauley was contacted by the general secretary of the South African Council of Churches, Dr Frank Chikane, to join him and a church delegation to visit the scene of the slaughter and to comfort the distraught families.

Some 36 hours after the shooting, Ray joined a church delegation that included Archbishop Tutu, and after a brief service in a local church in Boipatong the leaders visited the shacks of the people who had lost loved ones.

The sights were pitiful. When Ray approached the door of one ramshackle home, the woman, clutching a baby to her breast, was terrified that the killers had returned.

There were stories of callous killing and amazing escapes – like the young woman who threw herself through a window when she heard the mob smash through the front door. She cheated death, but her father and brother were gunned down as they lay on their beds.

There was little doubt that the mysterious horde of killers was deliberately trying to stir more violence. A bottle store, usually an instant target for unruly mobs, was untouched by the marauders. The accusations from the people pointed to a group of hostel workers who lived a short distance from the shacks. The hostel dwellers were said to be members of the

IFP. Those who died in the massacre were reputed to be either members of the ANC or the PAC. But even more sinister was the accusation that the police force on duty in the area had been slow to respond to calls for help and were in collusion with the killers.

The Boipatong Massacre headlines flashed around the world and placed the country on a knife's edge.

Returning from Boipatong, Ray issued a brief media statement in which he said:

'I have been deeply shocked by another callous and cowardly act of violence. I appeal to President de Klerk and the Minister of Police to take strong steps to ensure that such an act will not happen again. This mindless killing must stop.

'On behalf of Pentecostal Christians we extend our prayers of comfort for the bereaved and suffering.

'For the perpetrators of this horrendous act we pray that they will be conscience-stricken by this needless taking of sacred, human lives and will lay down their killing weapons.'

President de Klerk, in an attempt to appease the people and prove that he was in control of the police force, also visited Boipatong. Unlike the churchmen, who had been welcomed with deep respect and appreciation, President de Klerk found himself confronted by an ugly, hostile crowd. His motor vehicle was mobbed and he had to be whisked away to safety. Some shootings occurred and fatalities were reported.

Moved by the apparent impotence of the government and by Buthelezi's perceived intransigence, Ray sent a fax to President de Klerk which was also released to the media:

Sir,
    Warm Christian greetings.
    It is with deep concern that I appeal to you to do everything within your power to curtail the spiral of violence.

I visited Boipatong on Friday afternoon and spoke to many bereaved residents and prayed with them.

Having heard their first-hand accounts of what happened, I am deeply disturbed because it appears that the police failed in their primary duty of protecting innocent citizens.

There is a growing perception among moderate whites and blacks that the allegations of police/Inkatha collusion are not wild political propaganda, but are true and that the government is, in fact, party to promoting violence.

I am not in a position nor do I have all the facts to make a judgement on such allegations, but I implore you to urge the police to do their job impartially.

The shooting yesterday, after you had left Boipatong, brings back memories of Sharpeville and the patience of moderate-thinking people is running out.

Having spoken to people at Boipatong, and after yesterday's excessive police action, it is clear the confidence in the police force is at an all-time low.

I pray that God will give you the wisdom and courage to take bold steps to demonstrate justice, and put the hopes of the people first and not the expediency of political agendas.

I pray that you will rise above the selfishness of political power-games and take urgent steps to restore some sanity and hope to South Africa.

God bless you.

Within 24 hours, Ray received a stinging rebuttal from Buthelezi, who faxed him a ten-page letter and documents. He was incensed that Ray had gone public on the growing perception of collusion between members of the police and members of the IFP. President de Klerk was not far behind in sending a copy of a document in which he outlined the government's position.

For a while Ray did not find himself topping a popularity poll with politicians. He also wondered whether all the energy, effort and personal aggravation was worth it. A sequel to the Boipatong Massacre was the funeral. Having become involved with an issue, it was necessary to persist.

A funeral in the black tradition is quite an event, but over the years the burying of anyone remotely connected with politics became a grand show. The reason for the stage-managing of political funerals was very simple. Because of the oppressive nature of the South African government, funerals became a focal point for black protest.

The Boipatong funeral was no exception.

Ray, accompanied by members of his staff, arrived at the venue for the funeral service – a large open sports ground. The coffins were lined up in front of the main platform and a crowd of about 15 000 people packed the ground. The service, which lasted for over four hours, was saved by Archbishop Tutu from becoming a rabble-rousing political rally.

Politician after politician took the microphone to lambaste President de Klerk, the police force and Buthelezi. In fact, the anger of the crowd became alarming; it was not helped by a strong police presence, including a circling helicopter which kept a watchful eye on the proceedings. This simply antagonised the mourners.

Finally, it was left to Dr Chikane to bring some comfort to the bereaved and for Archbishop Tutu to bring a sense of propriety to the service. The truth, though, was that the politicians had hijacked the funeral service.

Sensing the mood of the crowd, Ray had no hesitation in deciding not to go to the graveside and instead returned home. It was just as well, because there were unpleasant incidents when some of the mob on its way to the graveside turned on whites and matters nearly got out of control.

Later that same year, because of his involvement with the Bisho Massacre and Brigadier Gqosa, Ray had another funeral to attend. This proved to be a better organised event and the service did have some church dignity. Ray was not only invited, but was especially asked to participate by praying for loved ones and for the general situation in the nation. These incidents illustrate one important factor: there is a price to pay for being involved in national issues. Sometimes it can be a very high price, as was the case with the late Professor Johan Heyns of the Dutch Reformed Church. This astute theologian and forward-thinking man held a pivotal position in his church denomination when it made a serious shift away from apartheid. From the late 1980s onward Professor Heyns was in the vanguard of Dutch Reformed Church leaders, willing to confess the failure of apartheid. But more than that, he was willing to admit its moral and biblical bankruptcy.

Ray first met with Professor Heyns in 1988. Over the next six years they became friends and close allies in the role of the church in the changing socio-political events in South Africa.

It was at a private dinner party in April 1991 that Heyns, Chikane and Ray committed themselves to a quest for peace which ultimately led to the National Peace Accord. This unique document managed to get the major political parties to pledge themselves to seeking peace through negotiation.

During this time, Heyns received many death threats from extreme right-wing groups who saw him as a traitor of the Afrikaner people. However, none of the threats came to anything and, as Heyns drifted out of public spotlight, it seemed that he would soon be enjoying a well-earned retirement.

It came as a terrible shock to the nation and to his many friends when he was assassinated on 5 November 1994. A sharpshooter cut him down as he sat in his lounge with his wife and grandchildren. No organisation claimed responsibility for the assassination and police still have an open docket. The speculation is that the killer belongs to a fanatical religious sect who believes Heyns sold his Christian birthright to a supposedly Marxist-inspired black government.

It is not only individual church leaders who faced physical danger, as was illustrated by the cold-hearted attack on an evangelical church in Cape Town in July 1993. The attack on the St James Church, which claimed the lives of 11 people, was not the result of the pastor's or congregation's direct involvement in political matters. It was part of the madness that pervaded the minds of some extreme political groups that wanted to sow fear and pandemonium in the hearts of the white population.

In response to this brutal and bloody attack when gunmen stormed into the church spraying the congregation with bullets and handgrenades, Ray made an urgent plea for peace and calm. In a press release he stated:

> 'The average South African is sick and tired of the continual killings, whether on the East Rand, in Natal or Cape Town. People are saying "enough is enough".
>
> 'It is time for the good people of South Africa to rise and demonstrate their desire for peace and harmony.
>
> 'A great opportunity for thousands of people to demonstrate this will be at the "Music for Peace" concert which we are organising at the Wanderers cricket stadium on Sunday, 15 August. We expect 30 000 or more people to make a statement for peace and tell the wild dogs of war that they will not stampede our nation into fear and more violence.
>
> 'It takes real courage to make peace. Only fools resort to violence to get their own selfish ways.
>
> 'Appeals for peace by political leaders do not appear to get results and it is up to the church to take the lead in defusing the situation in South Africa.
>
> 'The church is far better equipped for peacemaking because that is our job.'

Two weeks later, nearly 50 000 South Africans gathered at the Wanderers stadium in Johannesburg to make a mighty statement for peace.

The peace rally was the largest ever organised in the country. With the untiring work of Chris Lodewyk, the event proved a wonderful success, especially with the presence of the president-in-waiting, Nelson Mandela.

The church poignantly played its role as peacemaker and sought reconciliation at every opportunity, despite the threats of violence and fear that often swept the nation. This was Christianity at work on the coal-face of everyday life.

A pastor cannot expect to influence his community, town,

city or nation if he is not prepared to give of his time and energy and go to where the action is. Sometimes it can be at personal peril. More pastors need to get down from the pulpit and into the streets, and be prepared to face frustration, sometimes apparent failure and even rejection.

Ray McCauley's success in the South African socio-political field is based on a few simple principles:

- ❏ A commitment to making a difference for God;
- ❏ To look at national issues and be prepared to give godly input;
- ❏ To overcome the frustrations of apparently not making headway and being misunderstood at times; and
- ❏ A supportive staff that can put the nuts and bolts together and make a plan work.

But there are sometimes rewards and recognition that the church is a ready and able servant. For example, on the eve of the election in April 1994 the electoral committee found itself in urgent need of more staff to manage the polling booths. Christians from various denominations responded to the call.

A hastily convened training session of over 700 volunteers was held in the Rhema Church auditorium. Rhema supplied over 200 volunteers who were dispatched to different areas of the country. Many of these teams worked long, arduous hours. There were reports of Rhema team leaders taking charge of counting stations, like the one in Bethlehem, where Rhema's youth pastor, Louis Carsons, was called out at three o'clock in the morning to resolve a sensitive political issue.

Rhema's project planner, Chris Lodewyk, described the church's involvement as:

'... [a] remarkable feat and our people played a vital part in hundreds of voting stations. In some cases their involvement was to calm tempers and actually call people to prayer. At other times it was to physically help and occasionally to actually take control of the stations to ensure the process was free and fair ... it was a thrill for all of us to be a part of this historical event in the country. It is a memory I will always treasure.'

Such involvement in the affairs of a nation do not come easily. However, they provide outstanding opportunities to make the gospel relevant and meaningful to many who think that Christianity only exists behind stained-glass windows.

4   WHO LEGISLATES MORALITY?

It has been suggested that the church holds, or should hold, a monopoly on morality. The church, correctly, feels that it is the custodian of a nation's moral life. This concept was hardly challenged in previous centuries, and even for part of the 20th century, nations have looked to the church for moral guidance. But since World War II there has been a decline in the authority of the church which has noticeably resulted in a deterioration in the moral standards.

New thoughts, some parading as progressive and liberating, have mingled into societies around the world. New Age, which is really an upmarket tag for many ancient mystiques of the Orient, has tended to become the vogue, especially in western society.

The church, once resplendent in power and veneration in Europe, has been relegated to a tourist attraction for people interested in ancient buildings. In many parts of Western Europe the church is dismissed to virtual museum status.

Chuck Colson, an American writer, describes the age we live in as a post-Christian era. Certainly, in some parts of the globe that may well be true, especially in the so-called western culture. However, Christianity is still very much alive and thriving in South America, Africa and, of course, in numerous parts of Asia. The opening up of Eastern Europe and the dismantling of the former Soviet empire has created wonderful new opportunities to spread the gospel.

Despite the setbacks that Christianity may be suffering in the developed countries of the world, it is still the guardian of the morals which make up the backbone of family and nations. In South Africa the church has great opportunities to make significant inroads into the creation of the new post-apartheid morality. It is a once-in-a-lifetime possibility. But South Africa, shaking off the restrictive shackles of racist legislation and the dominant Christian conservatism of Calvinism, is now hell-bent on freedom at any price.

The trumpeting for political freedom has been heard and answered. However, with it is a Trojan horse. Under the guise of freedom of expression and freedom of choice, the pornography, gambling, legalisation of prostitution and pro-abortion brigade have taken up their banners.

Along with disclosures of gross unethical practises by the past government and corruption by past and present politicians, the future is worrying Christians – particularly so because some of the past deeds were committed by active church-goers!

These concerns are very real for South African Christians and some are determined to speak out on moral issues. However, it is important that South African Christians are not selective, as they were in the past, in campaigning for moral change.

The abortion, pornography, gay rights and other obvious issues are the ones targeted by concerned evangelical Christians. However, in a nation with six-million (out of a work force of 22-million) unemployed and the streets of the major cities refuge to thousands of homeless children, the evangelical church needs to engage in these matters as well. The church needs to balance its public policy concerns with a profound commitment to love and care for the rejects of South African society.

One of the myths that it needs to settle within its own walls is the notion that morality cannot be legislated. This is an argument often put forward by politicians who try to fob off the church with this answer. The truth is: whatever legislation is passed in Parliament does, in fact, carry principles and a value system. It is impossible to make laws without having a view of life and that must include a view of morality.

All religious beliefs have a value system that has a moral view. Even an atheist has a value system and a moral view. The reference may not always be the Bible, but morality is encapsulated in the laws of a nation. Therefore legislators should not be allowed to silence the voice of the church when it comes to law-making. It is true that a government cannot legislate spirituality or righteousness because these are functions of the Holy Spirit working in the hearts of people. But the State must listen to the conscience of the people and that conscience is best recognised within the institution known as the church.

The question arises: whose morality is legislated? The critics of the church and its moral views will argue that Christians are trying to force their lifestyle upon them and that it is undemocratic. It is at this point that many Christians begin to back off. However, it is not the gospel' or salvation which is being forced on people – to do that would be wrong and it would not work.

However, the church has a valid and tried moral code which has stood the test of centuries. New ideas and concepts keep emerging, but people, generally, fall back on the so-called old-fashioned morality. Christians should not be afraid of forming alliances with other religions which expound ethics and lifestyles which do not conflict with those of the Bible. Accordingly, the church should be vigilant in scrutinizing legislation. If it backs off from the issues, it will permit people with purely secular concepts to write and enforce the laws and it will be their moral views which will permeate society. What, then, are the key moral issues which distress so many South African Christians and others throughout the world?

Abortion

Abortion on demand is a major issue. The previous apartheid government made abortion a criminal act, although abortions could be performed in special cases, such as incest, rape or when the mother's life was in danger.

However, the ANC-controlled government which came to power in April 1994, has a very open view on the abortion matter and many of its senior cabinet ministers and officials favour abortion on demand.

The persuasive argument for this line, and this needs to be understood in the context of Third World thinking, is that too many children are being born into already poor and malnourished families. It is a desperate and real situation for mothers who have already borne five, six or more children to find themselves pregnant once again. They know that they cannot provide, materially or physically, for that child and so they resort to a primitive abortion.

From a medical point of view there is also a strong lobby to allow abortion on demand because of the number of illegal abortions which are causing serious health hazards to the mothers.

The arguments for abortion in Africa are compelling. Over-population, hunger and poverty are realities in parts of South Africa. The AIDS epidemic is causing havoc, with HIV-positive babies being born every day. This prompts further pressure for legalising abortion. Urbanisation is placing greater strain on living space and on health resources. One recent estimate put the number of squatters moving into the greater Johannesburg area at 1 000 people every day.

How can the church respond to such a gigantic problem? It cannot simply quote 'thou shalt not'. The church has to become relevant and get genuinely involved in the poverty issue if it is to sway abortion legislation.

The church, in its stand against abortion, which has always been championed by the Roman Catholics, is based on the premise of protecting the life of the unborn child. This, of course, has sound biblical support.

The charge, again, from the pro-choice group has been that the church is trying to ram religion down the throats of people. This is not completely true. The church has taken a stand on behalf of the unborn child, not only on a scriptural basis, but also on ethical and emotional reasoning.

The ethics of abortion are becoming more sinister and complicated because of the deliberate 'harvesting' of foetus parts for medical experimentation. Foetal tissue is being used to treat Parkinson's disease and the possibilities for using organs and parts from the unborn is opening new medical arenas.

The abortion debate, therefore, is changing. It is no longer simply an issue of protecting and preserving the life of an unborn child. If the foetus is going to be regarded as 'non-human' and not entitled to protection, the unborn will simply be seen and used as a means of generating spare parts for ailing and diseased living humans. It is a hideous scenario and the frightening question is: where will it lead us?

A disappointing factor in the abortion debate is that some church denominations in South Africa have not had the courage to make their position clear. They have evaded confrontation by simply saying it is up to the individual and their conscience. That is abdicating what God called His church to be – an institute that speaks with authority and gives clear and righteous guidelines in times of confusion.

What, then, should Christians and other people who care about the unborn child do?

Some of the proposals put to the government by a national anti-abortion forum chaired by Ray McCauley included the following practical suggestions:

❑ The allocation of finance from the Department of Health for the provision of homes for unmarried mothers which could be staffed by volunteers from various church organisations.

❑ More accessible pregnancy crisis counselling centres for women tempted to have an abortion. Churches, again, could supply volunteer staff for this.

❑ More nationwide adoption centres that will give women the option of having their child adopted.

❑ Responsible sex education in schools that promotes sound family values and emphasises the moral responsibility of engaging in sexual acts, particularly in view of the AIDS epidemic which threatens so many people.

❑ A nationwide campaign to promote chastity among the youth.

❑ A nationwide campaign to educate men to accept their sexual responsibilities.

❑ A nationwide campaign to educate women, including married women, that they have rights when it comes to family planning. Women and teenage girls need to know that saying 'No' is a right that they have and that should be respected.

The following is an excerpt of the submission made on behalf of a group of charismatic churches to the South African Constitutional Assembly which formulated the country's first Bill of Rights:

'We believe that human life begins at the moment of conception. The argument that the unborn baby is not a person until after birth when it can experience emotions, is rejected by orthodox Christian beliefs. Christian belief is that the conception and birth of a child is not an accident and does not go unnoticed by God.

'We believe very strongly that a foetus has "rights", which are co-equal with that of the mother. This, of course, is a most critical point of the debate – when is a foetus a living person?

'However, if life is not present in the mother's womb at even the earliest stage of pregnancy, then what is it that must be killed, lest it continues to grow?

'And if the life is not human, of what species is it?

'Further, we cannot support the notion that the woman, only, has the sole right to decide what to do with a so-called "unwanted pregnancy". Pregnancy is not some mysterious thing – it is the result of two people engaging in sex and, unless they are both mentally deficient, they know that there is a possibility of the woman conceiving a child.

'As a church, we regard abortion as a serious violation of human rights and a contradiction of the most essential value in our society – the family. Some feminist movements choose to major on the issue of women's rights, regarding their own bodies. Few are prepared to speak up for the rights of the unborn child.

'The female responsibility for what she does with her body needs to be taken into account before engaging in sex. When a woman willingly engages in the sex act she is aware that she is running the risk of falling pregnant and is therefore co-responsible for the foetus. The male, too, shares this responsibility to the unborn child.

'We cannot support abortion as a means of birth control. In our opinion it is demeaning to womanhood. It may also lead to emotional guilt later in life. There are other, better ways of birth control available.

'Abortion is a symptom of a greater social need, which is to teach people about the sanctity of sex in marriage and of the responsibility of having children. Sadly, people often engage in random sex, simply to satisfy their lusts.

'It is sad that abortion is seen as a solution to promiscuous living. We believe that the lobbyists for abortion are taking a defeatist attitude regarding the moral fibre of our society. This defeatist attitude only compounds the problems of society instead of taking a positive step towards educating people to abstain from sex outside of marriage and maintain the value of the family.

'Instead of using abortion to dispose of unwanted children, we should be educating young people about the sacredness and responsibility of sex.

'It is our perception that the male is often the one responsible for pressuring women to resort to abortions, and young males need to be taught respect for the noble virtues and rights of women.'

Diedrich Bonhoeffer, the German scholar, had this to say on abortion in his book *Ethics*:

'Destruction of the embryo in the mother's womb is a violation of the right to live which God has bestowed upon this nascent life. To raise the question whether we are here concerned already with a human being or not, is merely to confuse the issue. The simple fact is that God certainly intended to create a human being and that this nascent human being is deliberately deprived of life. And that is nothing but murder.'

John Calvin, the famous Reformer, had this to say on abortion:

> 'The foetus carried in the mother's womb is already a man; and it is quite unnatural that a life is destroyed of one who has not yet seen its enjoyment. For it seems more unworthy that a man is killed in his home rather than in his field, because for each man his home is his safest refuge. How much more abominable ought it to be considered to kill a foetus in the womb who has not yet been brought into the light.'

The church in South Africa can still win the abortion battle if it mobilises and is prepared to become part of the solution. Large amounts of money and resources are needed, but it would be worth the effort to make South Africa a nation proud of its family traditions and its respect for life.

The nation has experienced many years of violence and there is a 'culture of death' in South Africa which has lost all respect for the dignity and value of life. If South Africa were to acquiesce to the pro-choice demands for abortion it would continue the never-ending spiral of death and destruction.

If the life of the unborn were to be unsafe, it is only a few steps further for the predators of death to begin to consider what value the sick and elderly have in society. With the degrading of respect and value for life, the spectre of euthanasia becomes another challenge to the moral fibre of the people.

In 1995 the laws governing abortion were decriminalized and abortion is now more readily available in South Africa. However, the final Constitution has enshrined the words 'right to life', which of course leaves the door open for challenge in the Constitutional Court.

Pornography

Abortion is not the only moral challenge in the new democratic South Africa. Another threat which has invaded many other nations is pornography. During the apartheid era 'girlie magazines' were banned. The censorship laws, which were mainly used to restrict the flow of honest information from the media to the public, also muzzled the pornography kings.

The porn pedlars have not been slow out of the starting blocks. With media censorship now lifted, the publishers of pornography and other dubious material have been among the first to espouse the right to freedom of expression.

It sounds noble for publishers to claim their right to publish what they wish, and it obviously makes a new-found government feel good to be able to champion a free media. But should any publication have the right to distort the truth about ordinary human behaviour?

Pornographic videos and magazines implicitly assume that women are purely for the pleasure of men, and that women enjoy being abused, raped and tied up; that men are animalistic, driven by wild sexual desires that cannot be satisfied; and that sexual pleasures in marriage can be enhanced by watching or reading pornographic material.

The publishers of porn claim that there is no authentic evidence to prove that their material has any damaging effect on people. Then why does it upset so many people? The real truth is that porn is big money.

Studies conducted in America by the FBI Academy and by the Michigan State Police linked sex-related crimes to people who were addicted to pornographic material. The Michigan report linked 40 per cent of its assault charges to pornography.

No studies have been conducted in South Africa, but Christians have been militant in keeping much of this offensive material off the shelves of some of the country's major chain stores. That, of course, is the most potent force that the church has – its ability to mobilise a consumer boycott. In America, some of the slick 'girlie magazines' were taken off the shelves of over 12 000 retail stores because of the efforts of the National Coalition Against Pornography.

The key to the debate is the clash between two 'rights' – the right to freedom of expression and the right to human dignity. Some of the arguments put forward by the purveyors of smut are:

- ❏ We need the free exchange of information, expression and debate so that the best ideas will prevail in society.
- ❏ Because the use of pornographic material is mostly for personal fantasy, it would be dangerous for a government to try to control the private thoughts of its citizens.
- ❏ It is almost impossible to reach consensus on what is obscene or not because tastes vary.
- ❏ Censorship of pornography is an attempt to impose religious values on society.

Of course, the exponents of pornography in South Africa are taking full advantage of their right to freedom of expression, knowing that any tough government action could be interpreted as a return to the jackboot days of apartheid. In those days, the free exchange of information was blighted and every effort was made to control the minds of the population.

However, the arguments against pornography are powerful. Firstly, Christians wholeheartedly support freedom of speech as a basic human right. Pornography, though, has no right to hide under this protection.

It is not literature. It is not art. It is not scientific. It is not a medical text book. No-one objects to an authentic study of human anatomy being displayed in a medical book. Pornography is promoted solely for selfish, financial gain and does not take into account, nor does it care about, the social harm it causes in society.

In 1987 a University of Utah psychologist conducted a pilot study for the American Justice Department. The study was on children who were customers of a New York dial-a-porn service. He found that, without exception, the children had become addicted to hearing about explicit adult sex over the telephone.

Another American psychologist, Edward Donnerstein of the University of Wisconsin, conducted research into the effects of pornographic violence on men's attitudes towards women. He found that repeated viewing of sexually violent movies desensitized men towards violence and made them trivialize rape.

Numerous other studies have been conducted in other American universities. They come to the same conclusion: that pornography is antisocial. It promotes the victimization of women and is a proven factor in many rapes and murders. Children are at great risk if pornographic material is found at home. Children were often the victims of molestation because of the use of pornographic material.

In May 1995, a South African magistrate, in sentencing a 29-year-old man for child molestation, said he was sure a pornographic video of group sex had been a major contributing factor in the offence.

The interesting thing to note about pornography in South Africa is that it is prevalent mainly among the white population. The most prominent magazines have a total circulation of about half-a-million, out of a total population of 40-million people. In African culture, the sight of bare-breasted, scantily-clothed women is not viewed as erotic. In fact, it is not uncommon to see bare-breasted African women at official functions in the new democratic South Africa.

Christians in South Africa are determined to stamp out pornography or at least place severe restrictions on the distribution of this type of material.

According to one Christian media source, the reported cases of child abuse have increased by over 50 per cent each year since the relaxation of censorship laws governing pornographic material.

Probably one of the most glaring illustrations of the destructive results of unrestricted sexual freedom is found in Denmark. In 1967 the Danes legalized pornography, followed by abortion on demand, and removed from the lawbooks former sexual crimes like homosexuality, sodomy and indecent exposure. The 'age of consent' was also lowered.

This radical legislation was applauded in many ultra-liberal circles and it was claimed that sexual crimes had reduced dramatically. It was obvious that sexual crimes would decline because they were no longer prohibited by law. It was the same as saying that because murder is no longer a crime, there is a reduction in the incidence of murder!

However, the following facts began to emerge in Denmark: venereal disease increased by 200 per cent for those over 20 years, 250 per cent for those between the ages of 16 and 20 and 400 per cent for those 15 years and younger. The abortion rate rose 500 per cent and assault rape increased by 300 per cent. Illegitimate pregnancies were up 50 per cent.

More damning evidence comes from Australia, the United States, New Zealand and England. These countries relaxed laws on pornography and reflected a marked increase in rape according to a study conducted between 1964 and 1974. Australia's figures rose 160 per cent, the United States by 139 per cent, New Zealand by 107 per cent and England by 94 per cent. In comparison, Singapore, which bans pornography, reflected an increase of only 69 per cent, while Japan presented a 49 per cent decrease!

Can the distributers of pornography claim that it is simply an innocent pleasure? The exponents of pornography cannot argue that their movies, books and magazines are just for private, personal pleasure. The people who buy pornography are endangering themselves and are a potential threat to innocent women and children.

Would the government be making a moral judgement by legislating against pornography and be accused of trying to impose a religious ideal on the population? Certainly not. There are laws against murder, rape, theft and drunken driving; these are moral laws that all good people support. Therefore, when certain practises clearly and seriously threaten public health and wellbeing, it is necessary for governments to legislate laws that are both public and private. Murdering a person in public is no worse a crime than murdering someone in the privacy of their own home. It is wrong and against the law.

The solution may be difficult to find because of the freedom of expression clause in the South African Bill of Rights, but the publishers and the bookstores will get the message when Christians and others opposed to smut and filth boycott stores that carry such material.

Gay Rights

Yet another challenge is the growing case for 'gay rights' in South Africa. Because of the prominence of AIDS and the need to promote awareness of the dangers of the killer virus, thousands of gays have come out of the closet.

Unfortunately, the South African church has been lopsided in its approach to the gay community. Fundamentalists have resorted to the 'turn or burn' tactic, showing little love or compassion for the homosexual. More liberal churches have either embraced the lifestyle or retired to the prayer closet or ignored the issue.

Like many other gay movements around the world, the South African community is becoming more militant and demanding. The gay issue has gained more publicity because of a controversial clause included in the country's new Bill of Rights which deals with equality. In essence, the Bill prohibits any discrimination based on 'sexual orientation'.

In its submission to the Constitutional Assembly the 600-strong independent church organisation, the International Fellowship of Christian Churches, of which Ray McCauley is a leader, stated the following:

'We see the inclusion of the words "sexual orientation" in the present draft Bill of Human Rights as an attempt to entrench "gay rights".

'We believe that other sections of the Bill of Rights provide adequate protection for homosexuals and lesbians within our society.

'For example, "freedom of expression", "freedom of association", "privacy", "human dignity" and in the "equality" sections, already contain the words "... unfairly discriminated against ..."

'We believe that the special protection that gays seek under a Bill of Rights would only expose them further as "victims".

'The aim of a Bill of Rights is, in our understanding, a way of guaranteeing certain freedoms. But those freedoms often have a cost. Campaigns to assist people in being treated like others have a way of backfiring.

'Instead of merging into the rest of society, minorities are not only marked as "different", but are forever seen as "victims" begging for their rights.

'There is also, in our opinion, a false assumption that full equality of gays can only be accomplished by designating them as "victims". Their claim, it seems, is that they are discriminated against by society.

'This is debatable because of the following reasons:

❑ Homosexuals and lesbians do not, generally, suffer any discernible economic deprivation and already operate in all levels of South African society;
❑ They are not deprived of education; and
❑ They have equal access to jobs.

'In fact, we may be surprised to find that homosexuals are not only well educated, but probably better educated than the general population – certainly not the marks of an oppressed minority!

'Mr Andrew Sullivan, the gay editor of the American magazine *New Republic*, has noted that no "cumulative effect of deprivation" takes place with homosexuals comparable to the "gradual immiseration" of a deprived ethnic group, because *each generation of homosexuals begins life afresh in heterosexual families*.

'Our point is that gays are not oppressed in our society, nor deprived of economic advancement.

'The gay movement, unfortunately, chooses to display itself as a "victim" and a so-called deprived minority because of their sexual and moral lifestyle, which they deliberately flaunt in public.

'It is not simply their private sexual behaviour which is objectionable to many people, but rather the public behaviour and attitude of some militant gays that offends many people in the greater society of South Africa.

'A person's sexual preferences are not normally displayed in public. In all normal societies they are contained within the four walls of the bedroom!'

Also coming into focus now is the issue of gay adoptions and the following comments were put to the legislators:

'The natural family throughout history has been male and female. Children deprived, through death or divorce of one parent, generally, suffer some form of deprivation in their development. This may not be evident until much later in life.

'Most people who suffered the loss of a parent when interviewed later on as adults, readily admit that they missed either the presence of the mother or father.

'To allow homosexuals or lesbians to adopt children is wrong for the following reasons:

❑ It is unnatural and goes against the cumulative historical evidence that the best family unit consists of father and mother;
❑ It contradicts the normal sexual behaviour expected of a married couple and can have a confusing effect upon an adopted child;
❑ The demand by gays for adoption rights may have a very sinister motivation generating a new 'gay race'. Because gays cannot procreate, the only way in which they can enlarge their community is to attempt to programme young children, through adoption, into a gay lifestyle.

'The current section in the proposed Bill of Rights on "Children" states "parental care" and that means, in all normal societies, fathers and mothers.

'Further, the same section stresses that all decisions made on behalf of a child should serve the best interests of the child. The introduction of a child into the dubious world of homosexuality surely would not be in the best interests of a child who may already be suffering from trauma?'

This submission and many similar ones from concerned groups were all ignored by the constitution makers who have produced a document which must rank as the most liberal in the world today. It is a classic example of an elist group of politicians, academics and ideologists deciding what is best for people. Many of the issues, if put to a referendum, would have shown that the vast majority of South Africans were not as liberal or as progressive in their thinking and, in fact, places great emphasis on sound, traditional values.

Family Rights

A curious omission in the Bill of Rights for South Africa is any mention of family rights and, on this issue, the church had taken up the cause with the legislators.

One church group's submission stated:

'The primary building block in society is the family. In South Africa the family unit has been seriously disrupted by the apartheid system.

'Because of the primary importance of the family unit and of the need to restore the dignity and its importance in society, we believe a section on the family should be included in the Bill of Rights.

'The Bill of Rights includes a section on children and we find it strange that basic parental rights are not specified in the Bill.

'We fully support the rights of children not to be abused or exploited. However, the exclusion of primary parental rights appears to give children potentially greater rights than their parents.

'To rectify this and to enshrine the inherent value of the family unit in our nation, we urge that a section be included in the Bill of Rights.

'The following is a suggestion for inclusion:

'FAMILY:
'Parents have the primary right and responsibility to nurture, protect and prepare their offspring for a meaningful contribution to society.'

Conclusion

As can be deduced from the above submissions, the church in South Africa has been active in countering the swing towards permissiveness in its newly won democracy. To date, though, its voice has been muffled by legislators stubbornly pushing for more and more freedoms without considering the long-term social consequences. To what degree its influence will be felt is dependent on the faithful prayers of the saints, and the amount of practical, on-the-ground work to which Christians are prepared to commit themselves.

There are numerous Christians in parliament, but to what extent they are willing to stand up for Christian principles is another matter. Some may fold under party pressure and toe the line, which in some cases would violate their conscience.

But it is on these moral issues that the church needs to uphold those Christian politicians and not allow them to become political fodder of the party machine. In fact, the time may have arrived for South African Christians to form a permanent Christian lobby to act as a liaison between parliament and the church.

South Africans, as a nation, claim to be 70 per cent Christian. It would be the gravest of tragedies if the nation's morals were hijacked by a secular minority. It would also be a tragedy if the church betrayed the nation by not contesting the battle for its moral resolve.

5 STATE WITNESS

An area of controversy in many nations is the relationship between church and State. Many governments insist on a clear distinction between the two institutions, trying to separate the secular from the sacred.

During the drawing up of the interim Constitution and Bill of Rights for the new democratic South Africa, attempts were made to to omit the words 'Almighty God' from the preamble. Lobbying by church leaders and the wise intervention of the ANC's constitutional expert, Professor Albie Sachs, saw these words retained in the interim charter.

However, when the final drafting took place and was presented to the nation in May 1996, the words 'Almighty God' were absent. The preamble now reads:

> 'We, the people of South Africa recognise the injustices of the past; honour those who suffered for justice and freedom in our land; respect those who have worked to build and develop our country and believe that South Africa belongs to all who live in it, united in our diversity ...'

This is certainly a reversal of the interim document which placed the nation in 'humble submission to Almighty God'. As a sop to Christians and other religions, the new preamble ends with the words: '... May God protect our people ... God bless South Africa ...'. This deliberate ignoring of the Christian desire to have God acknowledged in the opening statement should sound an alarm bell for the church. It could be interpreted as an attempt by some within the new South African government to make the country purely secular and to relegate the church to the background. On the other hand, the old constitution of the all-white government acknowledged the Lordship of God and Christ, but in the running of the affairs of the State it proved to be mere lip service.

The argument against the acknowledgement of God in the Constitution is that the inclusion of Deity cannot be regarded as a talisman or panacea which in some magical way makes the nation acceptable to God. But it is worrying since the Christian church in South Africa was a central figure during the apartheid age.

Admittedly, the church was split over the issue, with one faction supporting racial separation while the other championed and campaigned for equal rights for all people.

During the days of apartheid the Dutch Reformed Church dominated in the government. It bolstered harsh racist legislation on scriptural grounds and persuaded its congregations that racism was acceptable in the sight of God.

Because of its cosy relationship with the government, the Dutch Reformed Church received many favours – they had easy access to the airwaves and received privileged treatment when it came to government funding of welfare and social programmes. The Dutch Reformed Church became a fat cat during the apartheid years.

In contrast, the more liberal churches like the Anglicans, Methodists, Lutherans and other historical denominations took up the struggle for the dispossessed black people. As a result, this section of the church and its black, Indian and Coloured sister churches were severely harassed and persecuted by the fascist-inspired security police. These churches were labelled not only liberal, but communist inspired.

The church found itself in conflict with its own members and even today there are sections of the Dutch Reformed Churches that refuse to accept that they did anything wrong by supporting racist policies.

It was the true, witnessing church that caused the greatest embarrassment and was a constant thorn in the flesh of the apartheid rulers. Despite jail sentences, wrongful arrests and even torture, the church remained faithful and did not waver in its criticism and condemnation of the unjust system.

Most members of the Dutch Reformed Church have now admitted and confessed their moral failure in supporting a prejudiced system. And the once liberal church is trying to regain its zeal for normal pastoral service. Many churches who participated in the struggle against apartheid are finding if difficult to revert to simply being a church. Their leaders are finding it difficult to swop the political robe for ecclesiastical garments.

As a result, a vacuum is being created within the church system in South Africa. The Dutch Reformed Church, because of its past sins, will probably take many years to regain its credibility with a black South African government. The liberal church leaders are tired and weary from the many years of struggle. Men like Beyers Naude and Archbishop Desmond Tutu have retired. Dr Frank Chikane, a Pentecostal who was general secretary of the South African Council of Churches, is dabbling between politics and the church and seems uncertain about his future.

The truth is that many prominent church leaders are quitting simultaneously and there are few really influential leaders on the horizon. These could therefore be dangerous times for the church.

Wonderful opportunities exist for the Christian church to be involved with the reconstruction and development of South Africa. But secular-minded politicians may scuttle the efforts of the church by trying to bring a clear division between church and State. Some try to confine the church to Sunday services and simple prayer.

Many people do not understand why some Christians were so adamant about the inclusion of the words 'Almighty God' in the Constitution. Basically the secularists argue that one's religion should have nothing to do with public life. They are not against practising faith, but they say it is a personal and private matter.

When a Christian uses a biblical argument in a public debate, the secularists protest, often claiming that the person is pushing religion down their throats. Of course it becomes very awkward for a Christian politician not to make statements and claims that emanate from his personal belief in Christ. However, a private faith that never confronts wrong or challenges immoral or unjust laws is no faith at all. In fact, a person's political life is an expression of values and religion, by definition, dictates their value system.

The other basic reason for the acknowledgment of God is that, without a transcendent reference, the State is capable of becoming a tyrant and a law unto itself. The church position is that government is ordained by God, just as much as the church and the family unit, and that these three institutions are the divine pattern for a wholesome society.

Thus it is necessary for the government of the day to acknowledge that its powers are, in fact, derived from God and that its role is not to interfere with that of the church. Conversely, the church must not interfere with the defined tasks given to government.

There is always an overlap between these two institutions, but the key factors to note are:

The church's responsibility is to spread its message and have reasonable access to anyone who is willing to listen to its message. That is what is meant by the term 'freedom of religion'.

Besides its spiritual ministry, the church must be free to exercise a social function, providing relief to the poor, needy and the sick.

The church should not only train its people concerning their spiritual duties, but also train them to apply Christian ethics to all areas of life, including civil government, education, economics and law.

The church should be the moral conscience of the government, calling it to account to the people when it oversteps the mark.

On the other hand, the essential function of the State is to protect its citizens by punishing evil-doers and commending honest citizens, to maintain a limited defence force to protect its citizens from foreign aggression and an impartial judicial system, including a police service, to protect its citizens from crime.

In addition, it must protect society from monopolistic practices and from those who could inflame and exploit man's lower nature for commercial gain. This, of course, is aimed at big business which is able to control market prices and those that exploit, for example, the pornographic market.

While admitting that the State cannot make wicked men good, it has the responsibility to create the conditions in which good can flourish.

While these distinctions may be defined, the church needs to be vigilant to ensure that the government does not attempt to intrude or impose too much control over its territory. This happened with previous governments and is a reality again because of the massive social upliftment programme that is required to restore dignity and prosperity to millions who were deprived over the past decades.

The State, by nature, seeks power and will try to generate its own moral legitimacy for its decisions. The church rightfully believes that it should be the moral conscience of the government. There may be resentment when such criticism comes its way.

Nevertheless, there are areas and opportunities for co-operation between church and State in South Africa, which could greatly benefit the people. These include education, health and social welfare, and the provision of housing and employment. The task facing South Africa is immense.

The expectation of the masses is that the government will provide. Because the new South African government has a bias towards socialism, it feels obliged to meet this expectation. It believes that it has a noble calling and obligation to provide for its citizens, but it could be the beginning of a slide into the murky waters of a socialist-style government that paralyses the nation because its citizens look to the State for everything. Already there is a strong sense of 'entitlement' among some blacks who are looking for handouts.

There are thousands of misplaced, homeless children wandering the streets of South African cities. The government rightfully wants to help them, but the danger exists that the benevolent State, in trying to alleviate the immediate and obvious need, could undermine the main objective of restoring personal dignity and the desire for honourable, personal achievement. Where the government is seen as the great provider, individuals tend to become lazy and do not pursue their purpose in life.

This, of course, is the open door through which the church can enter a productive partnership with the government. As much as the government can offer physical aid, the church needs to refire the souls of the people.

The pressures on government to provide good education, efficient hospitals and sound medical care are tremendous. Again the church, once the provider of so many medical missionaries and educationists, needs to inspire its congregations to take the church to the people.

The church has a part to play in the drive for peace and true reconciliation. South Africans have gone through dramatic changes over a very short timespan. They have been exposed to unprecedented violence and a crime wave that has made Johannesburg the crime capital of the world.

The church and State are two mighty pillars in any nation. Governments have sometimes been benevolent, sometimes tolerant and sometimes tyrannical in their relationship with the church. The church has never fallen. In some cases it has been driven underground, but governments have come and gone while the church continues its task of caring and preaching God's bountiful love.

Therefore it would be wise for the new generation of South African political leaders to have the church as its friend and not as its opponent.

The Berlin Wall, the Bamboo Curtain, the Soviet Empire and apartheid have all crumbled. The reasons for their demise are many, but Christians who have lived in these repressive situations do not doubt that the prayers of the saints were the prevailing factor.

6 CHRISTIANS, POLITICS AND POWER

A recent development in South Africa is the emergence of a Christian political party. It goes by the name of the African Christian Democratic Party (ACDP) and is headed by Pastor Kenneth Meshoe, a Pentecostal minister. They currently have two seats in the National Assembly and one seat in each of three of the nine provincial legislators.

The party was launched with high expectations. The leaders of the party and some Pentecostal and charismatic churchmen predicted that the party could secure up to 20 per cent of the vote. This prediction proved to be wildly presumptious.

The ACDP is the brainchild of businessman Jack Stagman and a group of concerned Christians. However, as he travelled the country promoting the idea, the fledgling party found itself beset by some strange hangers-on when it launched itself into the public eye. It attracted some 'has beens' from other political parties and, of course, a flotilla of fundamentalists who viewed the launching of a Christian party as the saviour of South Africa.

The longtime communist bogey that claimed Nelson Mandela would lead the country into some form of Marxist State was high on the agenda of fundamentalist Christians just prior to the elections. They saw the ACDP as a bastion against any communist threat and were willing to believe that this new evangelical, Spirit-filled Christian party was some sort of divine intervention.

Unfortunately, the ACDP got off to an unsatisfactory start and is still struggling to define itself as a political party. In fact, some of its members appear naïve when it comes to knowing what the role of a politician should be.

The ACDP is suffering from the same perplexing problem that plagues Christians when they enter the political domain – and even more so when they bear the title 'Christian' and are driven by fundamentalist zeal. The ACDP has the basic problem of not knowing whether it wants to be a church or a political power. In the process it crosses over into the territory of the church and tries to be the church. The result is that it fails to maintain its political integrity and does not carry the weight of the church behind it when it makes so-called spiritual judgements in parliament. It unfortunately plays directly into the hands of those who advocate a purely secular government for South Africa because they claim that the ACDP is propagating a religious message.

This does not mean that the ACDP should not stand for Christian principles, but that it should fight for those values and standards and portray them as the norm for the larger South African society and not for an elitist group.

One must give its leader, Kenneth Meshoe, credit for his boldness in standing up for biblical issues. But the ACDP needs to realise that it is being far too exclusive. In attempting to maintain its evangelical and Pentecostal purity, it is excluding a large segment of the South African population that would quite easily support many basic Christian tenets which are accepted as normal in most societies.

Politics is about the democratic acquiesence of power. For most political parties the basic reason is to impose what it honestly believes are the best policies and laws for the people. In essence governments seek, through political means, to control their citizens. This may take the form of a benevolent policy or may impose severe restrictions on the population.

The problem for a Christian party is simply this: bearing the name of Christ means adopting a serving attitude. In reality, few politicians and even fewer governments serve their subjects! The ACDP has a lot to learn about the bruising game of politics. It must learn that its primary function is to fulfil its civic duty and not to achieve spiritual goals. A Christian party has the duty and the right to bring God's standards into the public debate, but it must do it in such a way that it speaks for more than just an exclusive group of Christians who are perceived to have their own agenda. Any Christian party must remember that God does not align

Himself with a political party even when it claims to be exclusively Christian.

Some years ago, the former British prime minister, Margaret Thatcher, gave a speech to the General Assembly of the Church of Scotland that outlined the spiritual beliefs that guided her political philosophy. Excerpts from this speech offer some amazing insights into the practical interpretation of Christian belief in the so-called dirty world of politics:

> 'We are told we must work and use our talents to create wealth.
>
> '"If a man will not work, he shall not eat," wrote St Paul to the Thessalonians. Indeed, abundance rather than poverty has a legitimacy that derives from the very nature of creation.
>
> 'Nevertheless the tenth commandment, "Thou shalt not covet", recognises that making money and owning things could become selfish activities. It is not the creation of wealth that is wrong, but the love of money for its own sake.
>
> 'The spiritual dimension comes in deciding what one does with wealth. How could we respond to the many calls for help, or invest for the future, or support the wonderful artists and craftsmen whose work also glorifies God, unless we had first worked hard and used our talents to create the necessary wealth?
>
> 'I confess that I always had difficulty with interpreting the biblical precept to love your neighbours, "as yourselves" until I read some of the words of CS Lewis. He pointed out that we don't exactly love ourselves when we fall below the standards and beliefs we have accepted. Indeed, we might even hate ourselves for some unworthy deed.
>
> 'None of this, of course, tells us exactly what kind of political and social institutions we should have. On this point Christians will very often disagree, though it is a mark of Christian manners that they will do so with courtesy and mutual respect. What is certain how-

ever is that any set of social and economic arrangements which is not founded on the acceptance of individual responsibility will do nothing but harm. We are all responsible for our own actions.

'We cannot blame society if we disobey the law. We cannot simply delegate the exercise of mercy and generosity to others.

'The politicians and other secular powers should strive by their measures to bring out the good in people and to fight down the bad; but they can't create the one or abolish the other. They can only see that the laws encourage the best instincts and convictions of the people – instincts and convictions which I am convinced are far more deeply rooted than is often supposed. Nowhere is this more evident than the basic ties of the family that are the heart of our society and are the very nursery of civic virtue. It is on the family that we in government build our own policies for welfare, education and care. You recall that St Timothy was warned by St Paul that anyone who neglects to provide for his own house (meaning his own family) has disowned the faith and is "worse than an infidel".

'We must recognise that modern society is infinitely more complex than that of biblical times and of course new occasions teach new duties.

'In our generation the only way we can ensure that no one is left without sustenance, help or opportunity, is to have laws to provide for health and education, pensions for the elderly, succour for the sick and disabled. But intervention by the State must never become so great that it effectively removes personal responsibility. The same applies to taxation, for while you and I would work extremely hard whatever the circumstances, there are undoubtedly some who would not, unless the incentive was there. And we need their efforts, too.

'There have been great debates about religious education. I believe politicians must see that religious education has a proper place in the school curriculum. The Christian religion – which of course embodies many of the great spiritual and moral truths of Judaism – is a fundamental part of our national heritage.

'For centuries it has been our very lifeblood. Indeed, we are a nation whose ideals are founded on the Bible. Also, it is quite impossible to understand history or literature without grasping this fact.

'That is the strong practical case for ensuring that children at schools are given adequate instruction in the part which Judaic-Christian tradition has played in moulding our laws, manners and institutions.

'How can you make sense of Shakespeare and Sir Walter Scott, or of the constitutional conflicts of the 17th century in both Scotland and England, without such knowledge?

'But I go further than this. The truths of the Judaic-Christian tradition are infinitely precious not only as I believe because they are true, but also because they provide the moral impulse which alone can lead to that peace in the true meaning of the word for which we all long.

'To assert absolute moral values is not to claim perfection for ourselves. No true Christian could do that. What is more, one of the great principles of the Judaic-Christian inheritance is tolerance.

'People with other faiths and cultures have always been welcomed in our land, assured of equality under the law, of proper respect and of open friends. There is absolutely nothing incompatible between this and our own desire to maintain the essence of our own identity. There is no place for racial or religious intolerance in our creed.

'When Abraham Lincoln spoke in his famous Gettysburg speech in 1863 of "government of the people" he gave the world a neat definition of democracy that has since been widely and enthusiastically adopted.

'But what he enunciated as a form of government

was not in itself especially Christian, for nowhere in the Bible is the word democracy mentioned. Ideally, when Christians meet, as Christians, to take counsel together their purpose is not (or should not be) to ascertain what is the mind of the majority, but what is the mind of the Holy Spirit – something that might be quite different.

'Nevertheless, I am an enthusiast for democracy. And I take that position not because I believe majority opinion is inevitably right or true – indeed majority can take away God-given human rights. But because I believe it most effectively safeguards the value of the individual and more than any other system, restrains the abuse of power by the few. And that is a Christian concept.

'But there is little hope for democracy if the hearts of men and women in democratic societies cannot be touched by a call to something greater than themselves. Political structures, State institutions and collective ideals are not enough. We parliamentarians can legislate for the rule of law. You, the church, can teach the life of faith.

'When all is said and done, a politician's role is a humble one. I always think that the whole debate about the church and the State has never yielded anything comparable in insight to that wonderful hymn, *I vow to thee my country*.

'It begins with a triumphant assertion of what might be described as secular patriotism, a noble thing indeed in a country like ours: "I vow to thee, my country all earthly things above; entire, whole and perfect the service of my love."

'It goes on to speak of, "another country I heard of long ago whose king cannot be seen and whose armies cannot be counted, but soul by soul and silently her shining bounds increase."

'Not group by group or party by party or even church by church – but soul by soul – and each one counts.'

One of the dangers of politics is, of course, power. Governments need power to implement their policies. In contrast, the church operates in authority, rather than in the perilous area of power. When Jesus faced Pilate and again when He was being nailed to the cross he had the ability to call upon all the awesome powers of heaven to liberate Him.

One spoken word, the same dynamic power that created the heavens and the earth, could have crushed all the forces of Rome and confounded all the Pharisees and Sadducees of the day. Instead, Jesus chose to be silent and not use His sovereign powers. Why?

He was demonstrating in the most dramatic and extreme circumstances that justice supersedes the naked use of power. God, at any time in history, could have used His sovereign powers to crush the devil and all rebellious people. God chose instead the way of justice to achieve His plan of salvation. This godly principle has been much abused throughout history. Tyrants and despots have exalted themselves to positions of authority, using power for self gain and grandissement. Power without justice will ultimately corrupt those who wield authority.

When the citizens of a country allow their government too much power they could find themselves on the slippery slope which leads to tyranny.

That is exactly what happened in South Africa when the National Party came to power in 1948. Although its initial reasons for acquiring power may not have been inherently evil, it did not take the National Party long to acquire an insatiable appetite for it. The power that the government exercised was fearsome and many of its cohorts became a law unto themselves – to such a degree that certain secret police units began to operate under a sinister cloak of secrecy, buying and selling arms and ammunition, carrying out political assassinations, and perpetrating acts of violence on innocent citizens and then blaming these atrocities on black 'terrorists'.

The regulation and use of power became out of control in South Africa. Justice vaporised in the winds of self interest. South Africa is now plotting a new democratic road. In an attempt to constrain the powers of central government a Bill of Human Rights has been introduced. For the first time, the South African parliament does not have the final say in the making and passing of bills. South Africa has a Constitution which is supreme, and every citizen, in theory, has recourse to the Constitutional Court.

These are all necessary restraints if democracy is to succeed in South Africa. These deterrents need to be enhanced and honoured by government and ordinary citizens. Africa has a poor track record of dictatorships and abuse of human rights. Many African governments are awash with corruption and the misuse of finances.

South Africa has come out of a 46-year ordeal during which the rights of millions of ordinary people were ignored. The so-called Christian government of the past, besides abusing its power, was also tainted with scandals and corruption. The transformation to a democratically elected government, a miracle in itself, is only the beginning for South Africa.

The dangers of the abuse of power and corruption are real threats to the country's future prosperity. The church should be in the forefront of restraining the government in the excessive use of power and the abuse of funds.

7   THE QUEST FOR TRUTH

'Pilate said to Him, "What is truth?"' (John 18:38)
'And you shall know the truth, and the truth shall make you free.' (John 8:32)

Christian fundamentalists have two distinctive characteristics: they are usually intolerant of other people's views and they want to impose their truth on other people. On the surface this misplaced zeal may be forgiven. At the heart, though, is a dangerous defect in the make-up of this type of Christian.

It is precisely this intolerant, imposing attitude which has stereotyped much of the Pentecostal and evangelical movement and offended many good people who otherwise may have responded to the gospel.

Despite New Age, pro-choice, gay rights, pornography and the many other activist organisations that challenge biblical standards, Christians may have failed to recognise their role in allowing people to oppose accepted Christian views.

That may sound surprising, but martyrs of the church have spilt their blood over the centuries for the jewel called 'freedom of religion'. The church has always placed the highest premium on freedom of speech because it recognised the need to proclaim the gospel message.

It is the church, more than any other institution, that is the champion of freedom and liberty. Its premise for this comes from the Bible, where God clearly enshrines freedom of choice in the preaching and proclamation of the gospel.

God wants every person to be saved. Christ's redemption plan is absolutely inclusive. God puts before each person a choice between eternal life or eternal separation. God enjoins people to choose life. However, it is not imposed against the will of the person. Truth cannot be imposed – only presented and then embraced or rejected.

The unhealthy intolerance and desire to impose Christian principles on the masses is a backlash to a similar attitude expressed by the liberal left.

In most western societies, including South Africa, many of the institutes of higher learning, the entertainment industry and the media are dominated by liberal-minded people.

The secular media in South Africa took it for granted that abortion on demand would be allowed. There were very few anti-abortion editorials. Considerable space and coverage in the media is given to gay rights and the notion that freedom of expression and freedom of speech is a personal decision and 'if it feels good, do it'.

Unfortunately, when Christian activists take to the streets to voice their disapproval, they are often extreme fundamentalists. For example, when the gay movement staged a march in Johannesburg, Christian fundamentalists also took to the streets with their banners. The rhetoric of the banners and the remarks of the day won no points for the Christian witness. All they succeeded in doing was to further alienate people from Christ because they failed to show the compassion and love that Christ demands of His followers.

Evangelicals and Pentecostals oppose the gay lifestyle, but the task of the church is not to condemn but to convince sinners that they are lost and need a Saviour.

The Rhema Church has a special outreach to homosexuals and lesbians, and supports a hospice for people dying of AIDS. The efforts of these dedicated Christian workers has shown more fruit than the militants who wave banners proclaiming that AIDS is God's way of punishing gays.

Unfortunately, the liberal-minded media pays scant attention to the positive work done by the church in the gay community. Rather it focuses on the radical fundamentalists and proceeds to stereotype all evangelical Christians as militant and bigoted.

This impression, perpetuated by the media, is carried forward into other areas where the church makes a stand for righteousness and good moral values. The media simply dismisses them as wild-eyed Christian activists who want to impose their extremist principles on society. Sadly, this view is sustained because the extreme fundamentalists are usually guaranteed a voice in the media, simply because the news gatherers see them as controversial and 'good copy'.

The image of a large percentage of moderate-thinking evangelical Christians is tarnished and their input on national issues is often viewed with suspicion because of media stereotyping.

However, the seriousness of the matter cannot be dismissed as just a vendetta between the liberal media and the evangelicals. The issue goes much further, in fact, to the very heartbeat of the nation. There is a battle going on in South Africa for the hearts and minds of the people. The nation will fall either into the liberal-minded trap or the church will rise to the occasion to maintain the tricky balance between the excesses of liberalism which places the individual at the centre of the universe and radical socialism which reduces its subjects to grovelling slaves of the State.

The fundamentalist Christian view is not a contender in this struggle. Tragically, it is a spoiler which detracts from the influence and positive contributions which the church can make to the rebuilding of South Africa.

The broad mass of society is often confused and does not know which voice to listen to. Through the battering-ram of a permissive media and a government pursuing a distinct division between church and State, with support from the liberal academia, the public are open to coercive actions.

Apartheid's legacy of inadequate and poor education has left millions of rural South Africans easy prey to cheap propaganda. The ethical and moral arguments of abortion on demand, gay rights, pornography, freedom of speech and the relationship of State and church are subjects foreign to people still trapped in poverty and unemployment.

The bread and butter issues in South Africa are housing, jobs, food and education. Sophisticated debates on the ethics of pluralism, a secular State and the implications of a Bill of Rights and a Constitution are not going to win the majority vote. So the demand on the evangelical is great. It may sound very grand and presumptuous, but the future well-being of the nation could rest with the influence the evangelicals are able to wield in the burgeoning new South Africa.

That is why churches like Rhema, that have an embracing vision, command such prominence in the country. Despite the attempts to stereotype Rhema as just another pie-in-the-sky fundamentalist church, it has made a claim to speak to the nation. It is almost obligatory for the evangelicals in South Africa to close ranks and find ways of taming the extreme fundamentalists who prefer the Old Testament model of prophetic thunder, lightning and destruction.

Truth is the most sought-after commodity in the world today. Because so much of the world is living in a post-Christian era, the Bible is no longer revered as the highest authority when it comes to ethics and morality. That is the hard truth that evangelicals and Pentecostals need to face.

New Agers, liberal and socialist politicians, and a multitude of activist and philosophical voices are blaring across the countryside. They all demand to be heard, and because South Africa has shifted from a very closed, conservative society, they will now have the right to be heard.

Unfortunately, many evangelicals, like the Israelites who spied out the land, see only gigantic opponents and retreat from the battlefield. They are often more content to wander in the wilderness of suburban sobriety.

If the truth be known, many ministers and their flocks fear the cost of making a strong stand for truth and righteousness, as it affects society.

In South Africa crime and political violence has risen to an appalling level over the past five years; enormous peace campaigns have been launched nationwide. Tens of thousands of Christians have prayed for peace, but have all these prayers been motivated by the passion of Christ? That is a searching question for the white evangelical Christians of South Africa. Do they pray for peace simply because they want to indulge in selfish and comfortable lifestyles? Is it fear that motivates their prayers or is it a genuine concern and love for people?

The good news for South African evangelicals is that they can win the struggle to define truth in the nation. The fact of the matter is that despite permissive saturation of universities, arts and media, and of many politicians, the public, though confused, has not swallowed the bait of either extremes of liberalism or socialism.

The reason is simple. The 1990 census statistics show that over 70 per cent of South Africans claim to be Christians. Some people dispute these figures, but the overwhelming fact is that the ethic and value system of Christianity is deeply imbedded in its people. It is true that 70 per cent of South Africans do not attend church on a Sunday, but the influence of Christianity has touched almost every household in the country.

Why, then, is the authority of the Christian message under siege when such a large majority of the nation live by its tenets? Sadly, the answer is this: the Christians speak, act and look no different from their opponents. Christianity and worldliness, as defined by the Scriptures, have intermingled to blur the sharp image of Christ-likeness which is demanded of the church.

With this blurring of the Christian message, the vast middle-of-the-road public have been left without a definitive cause. Most are repelled by the ultra-fundamentalist approach. Because of an inherited Christian influence the liberal call, though tempting, has not yet been embraced. Socialism, therefore, becomes a tempting morsel.

And so the moderate and now clichéd 'silent majority' are open to manipulation by elitist cliques, from the right or left spectrum of society. They, the silent majority, want the truth. The evangelicals need only to mobilise a strategic plan and they could exercise a powerful influence in the land. Not just naked political power; not power to impose a so-called Christian government. God forbid. Rather, the influence to establish righteous laws in the land; strength to defend the poor and downtrodden; controls to curtail the greedy; authority to maintain a society that is free and tolerant, yet responsible and accountable.

Does this sound a bit Utopian? Yet that is the prize that is dangling before the evangelicals in South Africa.

PART TWO
SOCIALLY SIGNIFICANT

8 KEEPING THE BALANCE

Adapted from a sermon by Ray McCauley

In Luke 4:18–19 Jesus says:

'The Spirit of the Lord is upon Me,
Because He has anointed Me to preach
   the gospel to the poor,
He has sent Me to heal the brokenhearted,
To preach deliverance to the captives
And recovery of sight to the blind,
To set at liberty those who are oppressed,
To preach the acceptable year of the Lord.'

Everything that God does for a believer is, firstly, to put them in a position to be able to do what He wants for that individual's life. In other words, God wants to equip you with the ability to achieve what you have to achieve in your life.

In Colossians 1:18–19 (*The Amplified Bible*) we read:

'He also is the Head of [His] body, the church; seeing He is the Beginning, the First-born from among the dead, so that He alone in everything and in every respect might occupy the chief place – stand first and be pre-eminent. For it has pleased [the Father] that all the divine fullness – the sum total of the divine perfection, powers and attributes – should dwell in Him permanently.'

Pentecostal and charismatic churches and their leaders often find the so-called 'social gospel' unattractive. Some would even go so far as to say that it is not the church's responsibility. But if it is not the church's responsibility to get involved in social programmes, whose is it? The government?

Christians complain that New Age thoughts and other

dubious things are infiltrating society. Those values and philosophies will invade our communities if the church does not take its rightful place in social projects aimed at uplifting and helping people.

There is the danger of becoming unbalanced and neglecting the prime objective of the gospel, which is to win people to Christ. But if we guard against excessive involvement which detracts from the fundamental preaching of the gospel, social involvement becomes a dynamic force in the church. It makes the church a significant player in society and, depending how far it is prepared to go, it can touch the very heart of a nation.

The important key is keeping a balance. Jesus said it very plainly:

> 'Seek first the kingdom of God and His righteousness,
> and all these things shall be added to you.'
> (Matthew 6:33)

That is the godly pattern.

Some years ago the 'prosperity message' came into many churches. Some made it the centre of everything that they preached and, of course, it ended in disrepute. Prosperity is very much a part of the gospel – we need finances to preach the gospel and to touch and influence the nation. However, it is only a part of the gospel and the part is not greater than the whole. It is like the baptism in the Holy Spirit with the evidence of speaking in other tongues. Years ago a dispute over this caused a major split in a church organisation because one faction was adamant that you could not be saved unless you spoke in tongues.

This, again, is a case of taking part of the gospel and making it the centrepiece. Baptism in the Holy Spirit is very real and needful for Christians, but extremism only leads to further confusion. The result is that the world scoffs at the church because it fails to display the love and unity of purpose that God desires.

A story told about the great artist Michelangelo illustrates this point. One day the famous painter saw a woman in Rome. What attracted him most about her was the beauty he saw in her eyes. Michelangelo approached the young woman and asked whether he could paint her face, especially the charm he could see in her eyes. She agreed and the artist set to work on what he thought would be another masterpiece. He worked many hours on the painting and then pronounced it complete. He stepped back and dropped his head in shame.

'I have made you look ugly because I have over-emphasised your eyes. There is no balance to your face. I am sorry,' said the famous artist.

It is necessary to recognise that not everyone in the kingdom of God is going to run a massive social programme. We must guard against a judgemental spirit that will attempt to criticise leaders for what might appear to be tunnel vision.

The great German evangelist, Reinhard Bonnke, has one burning passion in his life: to win people to Christ. He does this by holding huge outdoor crusades in Africa and on other continents. It would be unfair to expect Bonnke to simultaneously carry out a social programme. Years ago he was approached by some German colleagues to get his crusade team involved in a feeding scheme in Africa. Soon Bonnke realised that the project was so large that it would drain him of time, energy and finances, and would, in fact, jeopardise his evangelistic crusades. He simply gave the project over to another ministry that was pleased to run with the vision.

The biblical basis for being socially significant is found in many parts of Scripture, but chapters two and four of the book of James give us a firm foundation for our vision.

James 2:14 states:

'What does it profit, my brethren, if someone says he has faith but does not have works? Can faith save him?'

This is a trick question, and James goes on to qualify what he means: if you have faith, others will see it. In other words, you don't talk the talk, you walk the talk.

James continues:

'If a brother or sister is naked and destitute of daily food, and one of you says to them, "Depart in peace, be warmed and filled," but you do not give them the things which are needed for the body, what does it profit?' (James 2:15–16)

These verses have a tremendous implication because they are addressed primarily to the church and are challenging believers to take care of the social needs of their own, first.

As ministers of the gospel we teach and preach its truth and ideals. In reality, however, we all miss the mark and some Christians get into trouble. What is our attitude towards them?

For example, what does the church offer a 14-year-old girl from a Christian family who says: 'I'm pregnant'? We are against abortion on demand, but what alternative can the church offer? And what happens if the family disowns her? It is all very well to lecture the girl on the temptations of sex and promiscuity and that abortion is wrong, but what practical help can the church offer in such cases? We cannot say 'be warmed, my dear, peace be with you.'

Because abortion is such a controversial issue in South Africa, I initiated a religious forum late in 1994 which brought together various churches and other religions opposed to abortion. This group, which includes Jewish and Muslim representation, is committed to a very wide strategy which includes lobbying government, a media campaign and providing alternatives for those seeking abortion.

One of the church's other concerns should be for the aged. And what about orphans? It should break our hearts when we see children with no father or mother, who don't have a home to go to where they can experience love and security.

James is quite adamant in 2:17–18 when he says:

'Thus also faith by itself, if it does not have works, is dead ... Show me your faith without your works, and I will show you my faith by my works.'

The greatest example of Christianity is to be a witness, to be one – not to talk like one, not to sound like one, but to be a living testimony. When people see God in you and see God manifest through you, they are drawn to Him.

Another powerful injunction to be socially significant is found in Matthew 25:31–40:

'When the Son of Man comes in His glory, and all the holy angels with Him, then He will sit on the throne of His glory. All the nations will be gathered before Him, and He will separate them one from another, as a shepherd divides his sheep from the goats. And He will set the sheep on His right hand, but the goats on the left. Then the King will say to those on His right hand, "Come, you blessed of My Father, inherit the kingdom prepared for you from the foundation of the world: for I was hungry and you gave Me food; I was thirsty and you gave Me drink; I was a stranger and you took Me in; I was naked and you clothed Me; I was sick and you visited Me; I was in prison and you came to Me." Then the righteous will answer Him, saying, "Lord when did we see You hungry and feed You, or thirsty and give You drink? When did we see You a stranger and take You in, or naked and clothe You? Or when did we see You sick or in prison, and come to You?" And the King will answer and say to them, "Assuredly, I say to you, inasmuch as you did it to one of the least of these My brethren, you did it to Me."'

Proverbs 19:17 states:

'He who has pity on the poor lends to the Lord,
And He will pay back what he has given.'

In our desire to be socially significant and to sow the gospel principles into the lives of young people, we were offered the opportunity of a long-term lease on a building in central Johannesburg. This building is not just any old building – it was once a despised symbol of apartheid because it was here that thousands of black people had to queue for passbooks.

This building, known simply as '80 Albert Street', was vacated and in danger of becoming derelict and frequented by tramps.

Because of Rhema's involvement with the poor and in providing feeding schemes in various parts of the city, we became acutely aware of the needs of the hundreds of street children who have found their way to the city. These children, many displaced because of the ravages of apartheid and in more recent times by the high level of violence in the townships, roam the streets, eat from rubbish bins and sleep together in huddles in alleyways. Many are attracted to petty crime and involved in sex and drug abuse.

Seeing a great need, Rhema jumped at the opportunity to lease 80 Albert Street and turn it into a home for street children. The Johannesburg City Council committed themselves to renovate and convert the facility to include kitchens, bedrooms and bathrooms, and run a municipal health clinic on the ground floor.

So far more than 100 boys between the ages of seven and 18 have made their home at the Paradise for Street Children, run by Rhema Bible Church. Drug rehabilitation is one of the immediate programmes for most of the boys are addicted to glue-sniffing. Many have been subjected to homosexual abuse. Other programmes include literacy training and schooling, community rehabilitation and life-skills training.

One of the aims of the Paradise for Street Children project is to create a Christian environment of trust where the children can receive discipline and counsel, schooling and training in social skills. The ultimate objective is to reunite the children with their parents so they can participate in a normal, healthy family relationship.

A manager and house-mother oversee the boys with the help of 20 volunteers from our church.

We have been blessed by the good reports resulting from this project and to see how these children are responding to Christian love and care.

The opportunity for the congregation's further involvement was demonstrated during the Christmas season when ten young boys were taken in by Rhema families and given the happiest Christmas of their lives. Another 20 were taken on a camping trip and eight children were reunited with their families. One of the Rhema home fellowships provided money for clothing.

This is the gospel in action. Don't tell me what you are – I want to see it!

In 2 Corinthians 9:8 we read:

> 'God is able to make all grace abound toward you, that you [may] always have all sufficiency in all things.'

God wants to bless you so you can help others. God may call a businessperson to prosper and succeed financially, but don't criticise that person for not going out to feed the poor or join an outreach programme on the streets. Their place in the kingdom of God is to provide finance for these projects. Or it might be a person with certain skills, like teaching, nursing or coaching sports.

When we became involved in Alexandra township, one of the oldest and most pitiful black areas in Johannesburg, we knew we had to provide a sporting outlet for the young people who came to our centre. We bought an old factory and converted it into a community centre. It provides temporary accommodation for the destitute; literacy and other life-skills are taught during the day and the youth needed a place where they could have some fun.

A good friend of mine, Dave van der Merwe, who is the president of the South African Amateur Wrestling Organisation, offered his help and skills. We put in a wrestling mat and he provided some coaches.

This scheme has been implemented at 80 Albert Street. In fact, Sam Ramsamy, the president of South Africa's Olympic Council, has shown interest in the project and is hoping that this wrestling club will turn out some future Olympic champions!

The key for all of us is to recognise that the greater is more important than just a part of the kingdom. It is not all just feeding the poor, or all sports, or all preaching, but a careful blending of all the social aspects that help us to build spirit, soul and body.

Don't point fingers at other people or other churches because they are not doing what you think they should be doing. God wants to raise people to be useful in different areas. We should rejoice that they meet some specific need in the body of Christ.

In Isaiah 58:6–12 we read:

> 'Is this not the fast that I have chosen:
> To loose the bonds of wickedness,
> To undo the heavy burdens,
> To let the oppressed go free,
> And that you break every yoke?
> Is it not to share your bread with the hungry,
> And that you bring to your house the poor
>   who are cast out;
> When you see the naked, that you cover him,
> And not hide yourself from your own flesh?
> Then your light shall break forth like the morning,
> Your healing shall spring forth speedily,
> And your righteousness shall go before you,
> The glory of the Lord shall be your rear guard.
> Then you shall call, and the Lord will answer.
> You shall cry, and He will say, "Here I am.
> If you take away the yoke from your midst,
> The pointing of the finger, and speaking wickedness,
> If you extend your soul to the hungry
> And satisfy the afflicted soul,
> Then your light shall dawn in the darkness,
> And your darkness shall be as the noonday.
> The Lord will guide you continually,
> And satisfy your soul in drought,
> And strengthen your bones;
> You shall be like a watered garden,
> And like a spring of water, whose waters do not fail.

Those from among you
Shall build the old waste places;
You shall raise up the foundations of
    many generations;
You shall be called the Repairer of the Breach,
The Restorer of Streets to Dwell In.'"

There are abundant Scriptures that support the church's need to be socially significant. The church can and should fulfil this social role without becoming unbalanced and neglect preaching the gospel of salvation. They are both part of the same message. The church's impact on society can be so much more significant when it rolls up its sleeves and gets involved at grassroots.

9 A MILLION HOMES

'For the poor will never cease from the land ...'
(Deuteronomy 15:11)
'He who has mercy on the poor, happy is he.' (Proverbs 14:21)

We have been warned by God: the poor will always be with us. In the new South Africa this has become a pressing problem. Besides the political changes that are rapidly transforming the social structures of the country, there has been drought, and because of past trade and economic sanctions, a decline in the working population. There is also the world-wide phenomenon of a drift to the urban areas. In some South African cities this has become a torrent.

People are leaving the rural areas either because they have lost their jobs on the farms hit by drought or because there has been no economic development in these country areas. The desperate need to find work draws prospective job-hunters to the cities. They bring with them wives, children and in-laws. Small shanty villages spring up overnight. Wherever people can find vacant land near the cities, they move in with their cardboard boxes, a few pieces of timber and sheets of galvanised iron.

There is no electricity, no sewage removal and no support system for these shanty-dwellers. Somehow they manage to make a life, but only at the lowest level of survival. Educational and medical facilities, transport and places of possible employment are sometimes still too far away. It all makes for a depressing and critical situation.

Cities like Durban and Johannesburg, and to a lesser degree Cape Town, have been particularly overrun by the flood of people moving into the urban areas. Shanty towns can be seen alongside the major freeways into these cities. The pressure to provide basic service sites is being placed on municipalities across the country. At these sites, limited electricity, water and sewage systems are provided. The difficulty, though, is to find appropriate land. This has caused great consternation in the once predominantly white suburbs where vacant land near their homes has been invaded by homeless people.

Land values drop and crime often rises because of the influx of homeless, jobless people into the area. The problem retards the process of peace and reconciliation, and of introducing harmony among the race groups.

This has become a taxing dilemma for many white Christians who are having their first real opportunity to deal directly with poor and deprived black communities. Many liberal and opened-minded white Christians have been sorely tested in their faith. Previously, in after-dinner conversations, they advocated integration and a fair deal for all people but now, when the issue is close to home, it sometimes becomes too hot to handle.

Late in 1994, a land invasion by homeless people caused a major row which catapulted Ray McCauley into the role of peacemaker once again. A group of more than 1 000 homeless people took matters into their own hands and pitched their rickety homes on privately owned property. Efforts to find a solution failed and the local town council took drastic action by dismantling and confiscating all the housing materials from the people. It was a tough eviction step supported by the local magistrate.

In retaliation, about 200 of these homeless people staged a sit-in on the steps of the town council premises. They camped there during the day and slept in the open at night. Some had small children and babies in arms. The weather was unduly cool for that time of the year and there were several days and nights of rain.

The matter became exceedingly difficult with town council officials and provincial politicians attempting to solve the matter. But no place could be found to accommodate these people. The larger group had dispersed and found living places elsewhere.

Moved by the sight of the children, several of whom were

developing severe colds, Ray decided that the Rhema Church should intervene. Rhema has a large property some 20 km north of the church, called Hands of Compassion. It is a place where poor, abused and destitute people are taken in from time to time. Ray decided to offer some of the Hands of Compassion land as a temporary haven for the squatters.

It seemed an admirable proposal and was greeted with open arms by the town council and local politicians. But there was a severe backlash from white landowners who had property near Hands of Compassion. They were adamant that the squatters would not move into the area; some even became abusive and threatening. But Ray stuck to his decision.

A showdown took place when the landowners threatened to blockade the entrance to the Hands of Compassion farm. With the media alerted and the politicians called, Ray went out to the farm to set up a meeting with the landowners. After some tense moments and a little jostling, he managed to persuade them to talk the matter through. After many hours of debate, everyone walked out smiling to meet the media. A quite remarkable and acceptable deal was struck which brought all the players together.

The Rhema Church provided the land and agreed to help feed the people. A joint committee comprising the church, the local landowners, the homeless people, the local police and the town council would ensure that the temporary camp was administered in an orderly fashion.

Early in December 1994, with hired tents, a group of 220 men, women and children moved onto the site. They were given a special Christmas dinner by the church and the camp ran amazingly well for the following three months. A few hitches were encountered, but the issues were dealt with through constant communication and negotiation, and no further nastiness occurred.

The operation proved the value of the Christian approach of love, care and a genuine seeking of peace and reconciliation. It was a very practical example of the church in action at a grassroots level.

Because of Rhema's involvement with homeless people,

and the experience gained from this incident and several years of feeding the poor, Ray initiated a proposal to the government to help house the homeless. His motivation was presented to the then Minister without Portfolio, Jay Naidoo, who had been charged with overseeing the implementation of the national Reconstruction and Development Programme (RDP) promoted by the government.

One of the key elements of the RDP is the provision of adequate housing for all. It is envisaged that over a million homes need to be built before the end of the century to cope with the homeless issue. The task is enormous and the expectations of the people are high, but the danger is that, despite all the goodwill, the government will be hard pressed to keep its promise.

The role of the church in this matter becomes a viable and exciting option, which Ray hopes will result in its long-term involvement in grassroots programmes. In his proposal to the government he stated:

'Besides the clear injunction for the church to be involved in helping the poor, we believe we could play a major part in providing practical solutions at grassroots levels. We believe that a difficulty facing the government is its ability to "deliver the goods" regarding the RDP. We believe the government has every good intention to make good, but that the process may take longer than expected to achieve.

'If this happens the perception at grassroots level could well be that the government is reneging on its promises and that money is wasted and/or misspent.

'The RDP needs the utmost transparency and we believe that the church community across the country could be mobilised to help improve the lot of the poor and needy.'

One reality already facing post-apartheid South Africa is the stark fact that, despite a new non-racial government and noble ideals, wastage and corruption still occur at government level.

International and local companies see some prize pickings to be made in the development programme that the new government wishes to pursue. Unfortunately, greed and bribery lurk in the corridors of both big business and officialdom. It has become an accepted way of doing business in many African nations and, if South Africa were to sink to the level of bribery and corruption of some of these states, the poor and needy will not see their expectations become a reality.

The need for the church to be the moral watchdog is critical. It can forestall much of the risk if it can work closely with and oversee social programmes aimed at uplifting the country's poor.

10 OPERATION MERCY

Besides looking after the needs of their own poor, there are occasions when nations answer the call for help beyond their borders. These occasions usually occur in times of national disaster, drought, famine or war. The cry for help is often answered by governments or major non-governmental organisations like the Red Cross, the United Nations or one of its many large auxiliary organisations.

It is rarely, if ever, that a local church congregation becomes the focal point of a national relief effort. But that is exactly what happened when the Rhema Church became involved in mid-1994 with an extraordinary mercy mission to the refugees of war-ravished Rwanda. It all came about by 'accident' but as it unfolded, it was clear that God was orchestrating the event.

It began when I read an article in a local newspaper that appealed for people to make donations to be used to send aid to Rwanda. Because of the tremendous burden of the poor in South Africa, the appeal did not meet with much enthusiasm from the public. But with the almost nightly television visuals of the anguish and despair of the people of Rwanda, especially the children, the Rhema congregation decided to take up the cause. Ray announced an appeal from the pulpit and food and clothing began to roll in.

Realising there was some newsworthiness in the response, the local television news department was contacted. They arrived one afternoon and Ray showed them a room at the church complex that was piled high with food and clothing. They interviewed Ray and filmed some of the goods that had been collected. Ray issued an appeal to other churches to respond and show compassion for the people of Rwanda.

That night he conducted a local leadership meeting in the main church auditorium. Midway through the meeting, he was interrupted by an urgent telephone call from the recently appointed Deputy Vice-President, Thabo Mbeki.

It transpired that he and President Nelson Mandela had

been watching the television news and had seen the short insert featuring the Rwandan appeal.

They had just discussed how South Africa could respond to the situation. Because South Africa was now welcome in the fold of the Organisation of African Unity (OAU), it was felt that the newly democratic South Africa should somehow be seen to be involved peacefully in Africa.

Most of South Africa's previous forays into Africa had been subversive or military. For example in Rhodesia (now Zimbabwe), security forces were used to prop up Ian Smith's regime. South African troops fought in Angola for 17 years and also in Mozambique, South West Africa (now Namibia) and Zambia. It was time for the continent to see the better side of South Africa's humanity and a mercy mission to Rwanda seemed a likely option.

Thabo Mbeki's conversation was precise. President Mandela wanted Ray to head a national appeal for Rwanda and the government would give it its full support. Ray was promised military and airforce backing, as well as that of the Department of Foreign Affairs. What had been a simple congregational effort would now become a national one.

Ray marshalled his staff and colleague Chris Lodewyk, who had many years of experience with German evangelist Reinhard Bonnke as a crusade and conference director. He was given the task of coordinating what became known as 'Operation Mercy'.

One of the conditions set by President Mandela was that the effort should be truly national and that the organising committee should be as representative as possible. This meant not only including other churches and denominations, but also inviting other religious groups to participate. The value of alliances and cooperation on certain issues which did not compromise one's personal faith was now a reality to Rhema. Within 24 hours, an Operation Mercy committee consisting of Christian, Jewish and Muslim representatives was put together. Within 48 hours, Ray led them to a special briefing and television session with President Mandela.

Naïvely, the committee and coordinator Chris Lodewyk

believed that the first airlift of goods would fly out of South Africa within two to three weeks at most.

Operation Mercy proved that the church has an incredible network which, when it unifies on a common issue, becomes a dynamic force. Churches across the country collected food and clothing. Supermarkets, pharmaceutical companies and wholesalers were contacted and promises of bulk food supplies rolled in. Food chain-stores across South Africa placed special bins at their entrances, encouraging customers to donate something from their daily shopping lists.

The South African media took a special interest in what had been initiated and what the church was doing across the country.

Within 13 days, a network was established and the task now was to get all the food moved from hundreds of outlets, villages, towns and cities to the central airbase near Pretoria. Unfortunately, the efficiency of the military and some government departments was not as slick as the church's ability to mobilise its network.

Ray became so frustrated that he sent the following fax to Thabo Mbeki; Deputy Minister of Foreign Affairs, Aziz Pahad, and the Deputy Minister of Defence, Ronnie Kasrils:

'Since President Mandela announced a nationwide appeal for Rwanda on television on June 17, the church, Jewish and Muslim communities have been working day and night raising aid for the refugees.

'We were promised the full cooperation of Foreign Affairs and of the National Defence Force, and on that basis worked towards sending the first aid off on Thursday, June 30. This was communicated to both Foreign Affairs and the National Defence Force. To date we have no indication of when the goods will leave South Africa.

'This is now causing embarrassment because the public, our many donors and the media, are wanting to know when the action starts.

'I cannot take the blame nor the responsibility for the

delays or make any excuses to the media after today.

'The enthusiasm, goodwill and cooperation of the people of South Africa have been magnificent and I have a responsibility to remain transparent with them.

'The media interest in the event has been tremendous and I believe that Operation Mercy could do much for South Africa's image – not only in Africa, but in the wider international arena.

'However, people are dying in the refugee camps while tons of goods are piling up here (which is causing storage problems) and it would be a terrible disappointment that such a great effort was seen to fumble because of government failure to follow through.

'Could we please finalise the first flight to leave either on Monday or Tuesday to ensure that neither the government, nor Operation Mercy loses its credibility with the public?'

The memo was to the point and, although the Operation Mercy committee got some action, it was still thwarted by red tape and a lack of urgency which gave the impression that some elements within the various departments had no commitment to or for the project.

This perception was not far-fetched because, although South Africa now had a Government of National Unity, the civil service, the military and the airforce were still, for all purposes, under the same old white control. Not all of these people were racist, but key people in various departments, who still resented the fact of a black government, had the ability to delay matters through deliberate go-slow tactics.

After one particularly frustrating meeting at military headquarters in Pretoria, I phoned the Deputy Minister of Defence to complain. He was shocked when I explained to him what was happening. Soon thereafter, I had an irate government official calling me at home wanting to know why I was speaking to the minister. But it had the desired result and Operation Mercy received the necessary cooperation.

On 3 July a statement was released to the media:

'Army trucks will begin collecting goods donated to Operation Mercy for Rwanda on Tuesday morning. The PWV region collection is almost completed, but 29 cities and towns across the country have collected goods until today (Sunday).

'We began the collection in the PWV a week ago in anticipation of an early lift-off to the Tanzanian refugee camps, but the South African National Defence Force, working together with the Department of Foreign Affairs, have set a target date of 12 July.

Approximately 60 tons of food, clothing, blankets and medical supplies have been collected from the PWV region alone, and this amount is expected to double with the collection of goods from the rest of the country.

'It has been an outstanding effort by the people of South Africa. They have opened their hearts to the desperate needs of the people of Rwanda.'

Prior to the massive airlift, which would take the goods to Mwanza in Tanzania and then by road to the refugee camp at Ngara, a Rhema team was sent to prepare the way.

Headed by businessman Mark Bruno, the team consisted of the head of Rhema's television department, Greg Chapman, cameraman Rob Kelly, David Hawkes, a New Zealander who was engaged in missionary aviation work, and a visiting medical doctor, Calvin Billinghurst.

The team set off four days before the first mercy flights and travelled to Nairobi from where they drove the 1 000 km to Mwanza. Their journey took them through the world-famous Serengeti National Park, but there was little time to enjoy this renowned tourist attraction.

After passing through the Kenya-Tanzania border post, they eventually reached their destination.

At Mwanza the Rhema party, who had decided to call themselves the Rwanda Advance Team, or RATS for short, found accommodation at the local Roman Catholic church. It was here that they had their first insight into the dramatic events taking place in war-torn Rwanda.

A local priest had started work among orphans of the Rwanda slaughter and, in trying to help them with their inner emotions and anger, had the children express their feelings by drawing pictures. The pictures portrayed much of the horror to which innocent young minds had been exposed. Most of their drawings were of soldiers shooting at civilians running for their lives.

In an effort to help the more than 80 000 children at the Ngara refugee camp, special international trauma teams were mobilised and brought into the area.

While waiting for the first South African flights, the Rhema team contacted the United Nations and other aid agencies in the area to make sure that road and air transport would be available when the Operation Mercy supplies arrived.

Back in South Africa, the Operation Mercy committee officially handed over 210 tons of food, blankets, clothing and medical supplies to the United Nations High Commission for Refugees at the Waterkloof airbase.

With the massive Hercules aircraft as a backdrop, Ray made a speech:

'This project is, to me, a miracle of the new South Africa. From being a people torn apart by vicious racists laws, we are being transformed into a new nation with a new heart and a new purpose.

'This has been dramatically illustrated by the incredible response by the public to Operation Mercy

'When Deputy Vice-President Mr Mbeki telephoned me after I had been on a television programme talking about donations for Rwanda, and asked me to make it a national effort that would be supported by the government, I did not know how deeply it would touch the hearts of the people of South Africa. In an exciting way, South Africans are now looking to help others and to fulfil the Bible command to "love your neighbour".

'Operation Mercy has been an instrument to bring religious leaders together to focus on a common goal and that is to bring aid to the suffering people of Rwanda. On behalf of the Operation Mercy committee, I want to thank the people of South Africa for their generous support and for the hundreds of people across the country who have worked tirelessly to collect the goods and to get them to this airbase.

'I want to commend President Mandela and his cabinet for encouraging us to make Operation Mercy a national effort, and for giving us the support of the Department of Foreign Affairs and the National Defence Force.

'There has been much behind-the-scenes planning to make Operation Mercy a success and we need to thank the United Nations High Commission for Refugees for assisting with the distribution at camps in Tanzania.

'As these flights leave for Tanzania, bringing food, clothing and medical supplies, we also send our prayers for a peaceful solution for the people of Rwanda.

'We trust that God will have His way and that leaders, who will trust in Him, will be raised up and bring lasting solutions to that country.

'The church in South Africa has played a significant role over the past years in South Africa and there is no doubt in my mind that God answered the prayers of His people when the recent elections went off so smoothly. I pray that the church in Rwanda will become part of the solution in their country ...'

The next day, less than a month after announcing the nationwide appeal, the South African planes landed at Mwanza airport. It was an emotional and joyous occasion, with the Tanzanian government sending a special representative to Mwanza to welcome Operation Mercy and the South African Deputy Minister of Foreign Affairs, Aziz Pahad, who flew in with the Hercules. After a series of short speeches, the goods were swiftly off-loaded and packed into waiting trucks. At the same time, a small media team and members of the Operation Mercy committee piled into three light aircraft to make the 400 km flight to the Ngara refugee camps on the

Rwandan border. The sprawling refugee camps consisted of simple homemade plastic tents, which provided crude shelter for over 350 000 people.

After landing at Ngara, the Operation Mercy representatives were welcomed by UNICEF officials who expressed their gratitude to the South African church for making this humanitarian gesture to the people of Rwanda. One of the planes carried vital medical supplies, and vaccines were received with open arms by the local doctors.

Following this whirlwind trip to Ngara, part of the team flew to Nairobi and back to South Africa while others waited at Mwanza airport for the second flight of mercy goods. These arrived two days later and the tonnage was boosted because the South African airforce laid on a Boeing 707 which had a larger payload than the military Hercules.

In all, 12 flights were made on behalf of Operation Mercy. It was not large in comparison to the international efforts of the United States, Canada and European nations, but it was significant for South Africa.

11 Voices in the Wind

One of the great fascinations of human experience is to attempt to fathom out the future.

Ardent racegoers go to bed hoping, as they fall asleep, that some special horse will gallop into their dreams and give them that elusive jackpot.

Many young women – and some furtive young men – cross the palms of so-called gypsy fortune-tellers with several silver coins in the hope of being told about the 'tall, dark stranger' who will enter their lives.

In Africa, soccer teams invoke casting bones and the application of magic 'muti' (medicine) to ensure victory.

Magazines, newspapers and radio offer card readings, astrology predictions, all geared to offering the enquirer a peep into the future.

It seems that everyone is trying to live in the future to escape the responsibilities of the present.

Many Christians may scoff and even condemn people who place such importance on fortune-telling and astrology, both of which skirt the circles of the occult. In recent years, some Christians, especially those of the Pentecostal and charismatic persuasion, have become just as gullible when it comes to biblical prophecies and the great event which the church universal awaits – namely the Second Coming of Christ.

A few years ago, a booklet of several hundred reasons why the Lord Jesus Christ would return on a certain date was widely bought in America. Some copies reached South Africa. Many people rushed to mature insurance policies, and sell cars and homes in a frenzy of religious fervour to cast off all worldly possessions. The date of Christ's predicted return came and went and thousands of people were embarrassed.

The author of the false prediction, though, laughed all the way to the bank, having sold thousands of copies and was considering a sequel as to why Christ did not return! A few years ago, a so-called Christian sect placed full-page advertisements in South African newspapers claiming that Christ's return was imminent. One of its members was reported as saying that the Lord's return was scheduled for 1995. Unfortunately, so-called Bible-believing Christians are dabbling in sorcery when it comes to predicting the date, be it only the year and not the exact hour of Christ's return.

This event, which will be the most cataclysmic of all happenings of this age, is at the heart of all Christian belief. It is a doctrine cherished by all sections of the church. Anglicans, Methodists, Pentecostals, Lutherans, Baptists all look forward to this event.

Secretly, Christians have hoped that this momentous event will occur in their lifetimes. In the New Testament we read that the early Christians were already looking for the return of Christ, even though His death, resurrection and ascension to heaven were events of recent history.

Predictions have become more common in recent years. Although the Bible warns against date setting and clearly states that no-one knows when Christ will return, there is undoubtedly a sense that the world, as we know it, may be coming to an end.

Despite humanity's great cry for peace, the nations of the world are perplexed by wars and horrendous acts of terrorism. Despite marvellous technology, tens of thousands of people are dying of starvation. Despite the ability to transplant hearts and combat disease, the ugliest plague of all – AIDS – stalks the earth, respecting neither young nor old, rich nor poor. Despite modern cities of steel, glass and chrome, millions of people live in rusty shanty towns and cardboard boxes. Despite our ability to shoot for the stars and explore the mysteries of the universe, we still fail to care for our earth, which is fast becoming the garbage planet.

Despite our advancement in hi-tech skills and computer knowledge, we still cannot harness the forces of nature which bring sudden calamity through earthquakes, typhoons and volcanic explosions.

Yes, there is a dark side to the present and the future well-being of humanity and this planet. Taking that into consideration, it seems reasonable to look for divine intervention to save ourselves from destruction. To set a timetable and make forecasts is not only foolhardy, but is disrespectful to the Bible. Further, it brings Christianity into disrepute.

Why are Christians, especially Pentecostals, obsessed with apocalyptic events? They have a fascination for exploring the end, which has made many authors and publishers rich.

In 1992, evangelical publishers cashed in by selling over half-a-million copies of books that dealt with apocalyptic theory concerning the Gulf War.

Sadly, much of this futuristic speculation is radical, sometimes little better than the so-called 'yellow press', which is often criticised by fundamentalist Christians.

What causes evangelical Christians to switch off their common sense when it comes to assessing world matters? Why are so many end-times books produced that are doctrinally and theologically suspect? Why do pastors and congregations readily accept so much dubious material and sometimes treat it with the same authority as the Bible? Tens of thousands of Christians sincerely believe they are honouring the Scriptures, yet they interpret world events and social occurrences in ways that essentially contradict the established meanings of the Bible.

Is one reason not that many evangelicals downplay the importance of intellect and the productive use of the mind? In their zeal to protect Christianity as a supernatural religion and the Bible as the revelation of God to humankind, many evangelicals have neglected their minds.

Fundamentalists, consisting mainly of Pentecostals, have been most guilty of this. Their enthusiasm for the supernatural, evidenced by speaking in tongues and the quest for 'healing miracles', has produced a breed of Christian that thrives on emotion and sometimes places dubious spiritual events above scriptural truth.

Despite a mushrooming of Bible schools in South Africa, the standard and quality of what is being taught needs to be questioned – particularly in light of the way in which South African Christians view not only apocalyptic events, but also matters of racism, caring for the poor, reaching out to AIDS victims and other social concerns.

Pentecostal preachers, famous for their sloganeering and rhetoric, genuinely want to change their towns, cities and even nations of the world. Unfortunately, much that is preached from the pulpit is frothy emotionalism that makes people feel happy but rarely challenges their minds and intellects. The result is that Pentecostals fail to grasp the reality of world issues and fail hopelessly to have a meaningful and positive influence on the events of everyday life.

A classic example was that of the editor of a Christian fundamentalist newsletter who sounded the following warning prior to the 1994 election:

'There are many indications that violence and interruptions will increase around the period of the election ... wise Christians will thus ensure that they have adequate quantities of consumables on hand to cover any emergencies.'

The following advice was included:

'Store an adequate supply of drinking water (in case water supplies are disrupted or contaminated).

'Ensure that you maintain a good stock of nonperishable food. If electricity is cut for a long period, you will be unable to store food in your freezer.

'Keep an adequate supply of cash at home. Remember, if electricity is off ATMs won't work and in a major disruption, banks (and shops) may not open.

'Are you on medication? Have enough on hand to carry you through the danger period.

'Keep the tank of your motor vehicle full.

'Have plans to care for your children if schools are closed.

'Do you have firearms for personal protection? Make sure your stock of ammunition is adequate.'

Anyone who read that newsletter would have thought that South Africa was in a state of war and pending doom. Sadly, it was Christians who caused some of this mass hysteria among those who feared that a full-scale civil war was about to break out.

Another ultra-conservative Christian newsletter commented on the election:

'With the coming elections the ultimate battle is upon us, the battle between Christianity and communism, between light and darkness, civilisation and barbarism. It is a contest between those who believe in Christian democratic principles, private enterprise, a free market economy, true federalism – and those who champion atheism, communism, strong central government and central economic planning.'

These newsletters displayed two glaring flaws. Firstly, the two editors were out of touch with reality and, secondly, they showed little real faith in God. Pitifully, many Christians were influenced by this kind of hysteria, including those who should have known better.

It is also worth noting that the editors of these newsletters were amazingly silent during the days of apartheid when it came to condemning the injustices of the so-called Christian government which supported black puppet churchmen.

Although they and their many thousands of followers and sympathisers could possibly be forgiven for their blindness during the apartheid age, it is hard to excuse their behaviour during the run-up to the election.

In reality, the election was a most amazing display of peace and harmony with hardly any serious incidents of violence reported. Millions of South Africans of all races queued to produce what even the secular media, local and international, had to admit was a 'miracle'.

When the counting of votes was over, the Christian fundamentalists were left with cupboards of canned provisions. It was laughable, but what was indefensible was the fact that no-one was prepared to retract their previous statements. Even more disheartening is that many Christians are still prepared to give such publications credibility. This is not difficult to explain. It seems that very few fundamentalists are prepared to use good, old-fashioned, common sense.

The intellect and the mind are not to be exalted above the Scriptures, but fundamentalist Christians need to acknowledge that the mind is important and that God gave us a brain which we are expected to use. Did God not create the human mind? Is it not through the mind that we understand nature, that we enjoy the arts, that we are able to advance science and create better living conditions? Is it not through the mind that we appreciate beauty and enjoy the intimacy of special human relationships? Is not through the mind that we begin to grasp a fragment of the majesty, might, power and love of God himself?

Why do so many behave like brain-damaged androids, allowing their Christian experience to be become a cheap thrill that feeds desires and emotions? Christ came to redeem people and to equip them for life in this world. Living in the power of God's Spirit and grace does not mean that we must trade our minds for a soppy, sensation-seeking brain that cannot deal with truth and reality.

But it is easier for many fundamentalists to parade 'The End is Nigh' placards and proclaim doom and gloom rather than build a house for the poor or nurse a homosexual who is dying of AIDS.

12 RACISM AND FORGIVENESS

What made South Africa so unique among the nations of the world was not the fact that it was racially segregated. Many countries still practice some form of racial segregation. It was that South African legislators put racism in the statute book. They made separate laws – one for whites and another for blacks; they gave special privileges to whites and denied these to blacks. As evil as this sin was, the politicians were honest and openly displayed their warped racial thinking.

It is extremely difficult for people who have experienced freedom of expression and an open society to understand the long-term results of living in a controlled, racial society.

Just as the question is asked how the German population could have allowed a Hitler to gain control, so many honest white South Africans are shameful of what they allowed to take place in the past.

Being born, educated and working in a strictly segregated society has a sickening effect on the thinking patterns of ordinary people. Children went to an all-white, all-black, all-Indian or all-coloured (mixed race) school. From an early age children mixed only with their own race. That was the breeding ground for deep prejudice. As white children matured, they automatically began to see themselves as superior to other races.

Children could not help but notice that blacks only did menial jobs. They were street cleaners, janitors and washerwomen. They travelled in separate, inferior-looking transport. They lived in small, cramped and mostly squalid conditions; they could not afford to dress smartly.

These were the mental pictures that white children grew up with following the birth of apartheid in 1948.

My close friend and colleague, Chris Lodewyk, is testimony to the havoc of the race laws of South Africa. He was born into a coloured family in Cape Town. His mother was classified white, but his father and the children were all classified coloured by the government. The early seeds of racial hatred were sown in Chris's life when his mother, her brothers and all the grandchildren were forbidden to attend the funeral of her father, who was white. Governmental race classification destroyed what should have been a normal family, dividing people of the same flesh and blood because of the appearance of their skin.

Chris, who came to Christ at an early age, responded to a calling to enter the ministry and began his preaching career when he was 14. He recalls the personal indignities and humilities he suffered from white pastors and Christians in the early days.

Chris relates an occasion when he travelled with a white missionary worker into a remote rural area of the Western Cape to minister to farmers and their workers:

'We arrived at the farmer's house at about six o'clock in the evening and, because I have a light complexion, the farmer did not immediately identify me as a coloured person.

'We were welcomed and ushered into the house. My white missionary colleague was very uncomfortable and asked the farmer if it was all right for me to come in too.

'Then the missionary told him I was coloured. The farmer looked momentarily shocked and then asked the missionary inside. He took me around to the back of the house, where he let me sit on a chair on the back porch. I sat there for almost two hours before I got some coffee and supper.'

Despite the fact that the house had five or six bedrooms, Chris spent the next few nights sleeping on a grass mattress on the floor of a tiny storeroom, with no electricity or running water. Often the cups and plates that Chris was given to eat off were old chipped plates and mugs made from old jam tins.

Amazingly, the many Christians of that era saw no wrong in treating a fellow believer in such an inhuman manner. Such was the depth of racial superiority among the majority of white South Africans – both Afrikaans- and English-speaking. Later, when Chris married and had children, he suffered much vicarious hurt. He recalls a time in Port Elizabeth:

> 'I began to face the effect of government policy on my children. I remember driving with my oldest daughter when she was just about ready to start school. We passed a beautiful playground. I can still hear her voice from the back seat of the car: "Daddy, just stop and let me run into the park for a minute."
>
> 'The moment I heard that, I was upset and tried to explain to her how sorry I was that she could not go in there.
>
> '"But why daddy, why can't I go in there? I just want to swing."
>
> '"I'm sorry, you can't go in there. Those parks are for white people."
>
> 'There was no answer from her, but you could tell something was turning over in her mind. I saw something small, but very significant. The next time she looked at a white child, it was with the thought: "You robbed me of something I could enjoy".
>
> 'The innocent white child could not answer for the problem, but that sort of reaction developed in coloured children. As a result, they began to see white children as oppressors who had privileges which they did not.'

These are cameos from just one person's life. Chris's experience has been repeated millions of times in South Africa. Appalling treatment has been meted out, often in the name of Christianity.

The miracle of South Africa is the lack of mass hatred towards the white population. In Chris Lodewyk's case he took the initiative in erasing the bitterness, hatred and anger from his life. He openly admits that he harboured those emotions for many years.

He realised, though, that the hatred and bitterness was

destroying him inside. In 1980, at a Christian conference in Johannesburg, Chris walked over to white Christian leaders and asked them to forgive him.

Over the years Chris, rightly, had castigated racial inequality within his church denomination. He had been a tireless and fearless campaigner, often embarrassing the white leadership. But in 1980, he decided that the love of Christ in his life could not allow him to harbour continual grudges and bitterness. In poignant moments of love and forgiveness, with many tears, Chris became a reconciler and a bridge who helped his former white oppressors to be set free of their prejudices and wrong racial attitudes.

Today Chris is an equal among equals in the body of Christ in South Africa, welcome in the pulpits of once all-white churches which previously asked him to use the backdoor!

When black leaders emerged to challenge the racist policies of the previous government, they were branded as communists and a threat to the Christian values of the white nation. Tragically, the majority of white South Africans accepted the status quo. This is not to say that they were all racist. But the success of apartheid, enforced by a fascist-type security police system, kept the whites away from any meaningful contact with blacks.

Lamentable, most whites never really knew or bothered to find out how blacks were being treated. Many whites, who espoused some form of Christianity, simply had no comprehension of social justice or the concept of democracy.

Because Rhema Church was founded in 1979, its entrance onto the public stage of socio-political issues came late in the struggle against apartheid. Initially, the Rhema Church's thinking was apolitical. Although believing itself to be politically neutral, it had been founded on a non-racial basis and its membership was open to people of all races. Without realising it fully, the church had already made a political statement: it was against apartheid.

Most churches and certainly Pentecostal denominations were strictly segregated into the four main racial components – black, white, coloured and Indian. At Rhema no such distinction was followed. Because the government had relaxed certain apartheid laws, it was possible for non-white people to attend so-called 'white only' churches.

As Rhema grew it attracted a sizeable number of black, coloured and Indian followers, and as they became active members of the church, they felt the freedom to challenge Ray McCauley on certain issues. One of these was the flying of the South African flag.

Influenced partially by the patriotic spirit of the Americans and the ostentatious display of the Stars and Stripes at churches he had seen in the United States, Ray had decided to give the national flag prominence. Mini pennants appeared on desks and, when Rhema dedicated its new church complex in June 1985, South African flags flapped in the wind from the top of specially erected masts. To the average white member of the congregation it really meant very little. To blacks, including Christians, who were becoming increasingly politically motivated, the South African flag represented only one thing – oppression.

After listening to the views of a black deputation, Ray decided to take the flags down and ban any official display in the church. The flags disappeared and hardly any of the white members were aware of the rumpus.

The flag issue was probably Ray's first deliberate political decision and it made him more sensitive to the black situation and examine the implications of the gospel in relation to apartheid.

Following his resolve to oppose racial discrimination where and when he could, without resorting to simple rhetoric and media hype, Ray decided he would never speak at a venue which was racially segregated. This decision came after he had been 'tricked' into speaking at a hall in Rustenburg, a hotbed of conservative-minded people who believed in rigid, racial segregation. Not realising that the hall was for 'whites only', Ray preached there. It was only at the end of the service, when some black people tried to respond to an altar call, that it dawned on him that they had not been allowed inside the hall. After that incident he firmly resolved not to preach there again unless it was to a nonracial congregation.

Another reason which caused Ray to become embroiled in the realities of apartheid was education. Part of the vision for the church was Christian education. It was ironic that Ray, with only a Standard 8 certificate, became the president of the nationwide network of Christian schools which mushroomed throughout the country.

Rhema started its own school. Because it was a private school and received a limited State subsidy, it was allowed to admit children of all races. This was, in general, the policy throughout the network of independent churches which blossomed in every town and city after 1979.

Although permitted to run a non-racial, private school, a minefield of apartheid laws often thwarted the practise of a racially integrated school. This happened to a sister church and school situated in Vereeniging. The Vereeniging Town Council threatened to close down the Christian school because of the presence of black pupils in an area and building which were for whites only. The majority of the town councillors were churchgoers.

The Kingdom School row eventually reached the Supreme Court in Pretoria and, on the day of the verdict, Ray joined the team of lawyers in the courtroom.

The verdict handed down slammed the Vereeniging Town Council; they lost the case and were ordered to pay the school's legal costs which amounted to over R100 000. There was much jubilation and thanksgiving to the Lord for this important legal victory over racism.

Since then, all racial laws have been expunged from the statute books. Unfortunately, it is not so easy to erase racism from the hearts and minds of people.

The school issue further baptised Ray into some of the harsh realities of apartheid South Africa. Like tens of thousands of other whites, Ray, although instinctively knowing the wrongs of racism, had until then hardly done anything concrete to oppose or end the evil system.

With the emergence of more radical right-wing political activists, another school row flared, this time in Brits, a predominately Afrikaner town situated about two hours drive from Johannesburg.

A local pastor, Peter Varrie, established a church and decided that a school was needed because of the inadequate facilities available, especially for black children. The intrepid pastor went ahead with a building and it was soon full of pupils who were mainly black. From the start of the project, he was warned by the local town council that they would take action against him. Varrie accepted the challenge.

The predicament for Varrie was the fact that the Brits town council was controlled by right-wing conservatives who were avowed separatists bent on maintaining apartheid.

When Ray heard about the clash, he gave his full backing to Varrie and authorised me to orchestrate a media campaign if it was needed. Although some minor media coverage was obtained, appeals were made by all parties concerned, including a highly-placed security policeman, for the matter to be resolved without sensationalising the issue in the press.

Reluctantly we agreed, despite great provocation from the Brits Town Council, which tried to intimidate Varrie and the teachers by cutting off electricity and threatening eviction. The tougher the opposition became, the more resolute Varrie became. Ray was determined to support him all the way, even if it meant revisiting the Supreme Court.

Ignoring threats and intimidation, Varrie ran the school, and hired a portable powerplant to provide electricity. He invited Ray to a special opening and dedication ceremony. Ray wondered whether he would find a lynching mob waiting to disrupt the service. The hall was jam-packed with over 600 people, including the parents of pupils and many of the townsfolk. Ray pulled no punches with a hard-hitting message that addressed the issue of living out one's Christianity. He directly challenged people who tried to justify racist actions with Christian beliefs. He received a rousing reception.

What effect did this have on the Rhema congregation? In general they applauded, although some white members may have thought he was becoming too involved in politics. The reaction from black members was not as jubilant as Ray presumed. They expected him to become more radical and champion the black cause and the so-called liberation struggle with greater enthusiasm.

To win recognition from the Christian family of churches has not been easy. The theologians often regard Rhema as an ugly duckling in the church family or as a delinquent child. Trying to gain the nod of approval from the churches has been difficult from all angles.

The incredibly fast transformation which has taken place in South Africa since Nelson Mandela was released from prison in February 1990 and inaugurated as the first black President of South Africa in May 1994, has been breathtaking, to say the least.

For some it has meant a hardening of attitudes. Although exceptionally militant during the build-up to the first one-person-one-vote election, causing considerable damage to life and property, this minority group has now slipped into almost total obscurity. Its cause, white supremacy, is an antiquated as old-style Moscow communism.

For tens of thousands of whites the change has been too sudden. On the surface they have accepted the inevitable, but their hearts are far from changed. In view of the 40-odd years of racial conditioning that has taken place in South Africa, this is not surprising, especially when compared to the United States, where despite years of opportunity to combat racism, they are still a long way from accomplishing racial harmony.

To say that there is complete racial harmony in South Africa would be dishonest. However, it is true to say that despite the years of racial conflict, the amount of goodwill and tolerance is little short of a miracle. This is in no small measure due to the amazing spirit of forgiveness on the part of the black population of South Africa.

Why have they been so forgiving? Perhaps it is because of the strong influence that the church has had on South African society. Perhaps it is because many of the leaders in the struggle have professed their allegiance to Christianity. The late president of the ANC, Oliver Tambo, who lived most of his life in exile, never denied his Christian foundation. His wife is a devoted Christian.

President Mandela himself, although reticent at times, has professed his personal commitment to Christianity. He demonstrated this when he received the 1994 Nobel Peace Prize in Oslo.

The involvement of churchmen like the English clergyman Father Trevor Huddlestone, Professor Beyers Naude, Archbishop Desmond Tutu and many others has, indeed, permeated the whole of the anti-apartheid struggle. Chief Mangosuthu Buthelezi, sometimes the maverick of South African politics, has openly declared his faith in Christ.

On the other side of the political spectrum one cannot dismiss the sincerity of many of the Afrikaner politicians, like the last white President of South Africa, FW de Klerk. Even within the ranks of the extremist groups, there is a reverence for Almighty God.

It is clear that the influence of Christianity is a powerful force in South Africa despite occasionally losing its way when it came to certain sections of the church. Therefore, it is only right that the church should continue to play a role in the rehabilitation of South Africa's distorted society. Its chief role now is to bring healing to a nation that has spilt its lifeblood for too long.

As democracy takes root in South Africa, cries have come from many quarters to expose the deeds of the past. Because the security system was so secretive, thousands of human-rights violations are known to have occurred. In general, the white community has been totally unaware of how many heinous crimes were committed in the name of apartheid.

For the victims, mainly black, there is a desire to know where and how loved ones died. Many simply want to know where the deceased's body now lies. Within African tradition, burying a body has great religious significance.

Just like the terrifying death squads of Argentina and Chile, South Africa bred units of sinister killing squads who arrested and eliminated possibly hundreds of political activists.

Ray gained personal experience of some of these matters when approached by Reverend Brian Jubber, the pastor of a small church in Ladysmith. Pastoral duties led Jubber to make contact with a certain Captain Brian Mitchell. Captain Mitchell, a member of the South African police, was arrested following an inquiry into a brutal shooting in a rural area near Pietermaritzburg.

During the trial period Captain Mitchell accepted Christ, repented and made a full confession during his examination. In making this confession, Captain Mitchell accepted responsibility for his actions which resulted in the death of 11 people. He was sentenced to death.

Due to a moratorium on the implementation of the death sentence in South Africa, he did not face the gallows. His sentence has subsequently been reduced to life imprisonment as South Africa has dropped the death penalty. However, he still hopes to be granted amnesty, as do many other policemen and security officers of the former government.

Ray, satisfied that Mitchell has indeed committed his life to Christ, has from time to time tried to facilitate his release. Mitchell, who asked Rhema to forward his confession to the ANC in 1994, makes statements in the document which are chilling yet reflect the mind of the apartheid era.

Since his confession was submitted, a Truth and Reconciliation Commission has been established, chaired by Archbishop Desmond Tutu. Hearings have been held in major cities across the country and live broadcasts of the proceedings have been aired daily.

The Truth and Reconciliation Commission is trying to accommodate the need to disclose all the ugliness of the past and to provide a catharsis for the nation. Its task is not only to provide victims with their first real opportunity to speak of their personal horrors, but also to get the perpetrators to come forward voluntarily and provide information.

The sinister aspect to these almost daily revelations since the Commission began in East London on 15 April 1996, is that many people in the top echelons of the police, army and even past cabinet members are being implicated in a 'dirty wars' campaign that few white South Africans were ever aware of. The Commission is in for a rough ride, because there are people who do not want some of the deeds of the past exposed.

There are pleas for amnesty, but some of the evil deeds may be so dastardly that the victims may demand prosecution. Thus many may not come forward.

Another potent and compelling reason for perpetrators not to come forward is that some relatives may seek revenge. Despite the huge deposit of goodwill and forgiveness that exists in South Africa, there are still some who hold to the Old Testament right of an eye for an eye.

Trying desperately not to have a post-World War II, Nuremburg-style trial which tried and sentenced prominent Nazis for war crimes, the South African Truth and Reconciliation Commission is grappling to find an equitable solution. One thing is certain: whatever the final outcome, it will not satisfy everyone.

Besides the need to know, as expressed by relatives and close friends of victims, is a deep resentment that many of the perpetrators have been financially rewarded and advanced in their careers. Men who were in the lower ranks of the police and security forces have received promotion in recognition of their work and undoubtedly hold very senior positions today. How many of these officers were involved in dirty tricks and assassinations is unknown.

There is another matter to consider. Maybe some of these officers did commit unspeakable crimes against humanity, but do their wives, children or family know about them?

As in all wars, official or unofficial, those in the ranks justify their actions by declaring that they carried out orders. From that arises another thorny question: how far up the rung of command do you go? A general may say he received his instructions from a cabinet minister, who may declare that it was a co-operative cabinet decision. The whole question is a minefield of moral and judicial complexities.

The biblical precept is to confess and allow God to wipe clean the slate. Past sins are buried and forgotten because of the redeeming blood of Christ. However, in the matter of crimes against fellow human beings, it is not always possible simply to blot out the evil deed. A penalty needs to be paid and indeed, when possible, restitution needs to be made.

One may find a partial solution if ways of formulating a restitutional package can be devised. The subject of restitution, although it is a biblical principle, is not often taught or practised in the church. It is strongly laid out in the Old Testament (*see* Exodus 21:30, 22:1–4; Leviticus 6:2–5; Numbers 5:7; Proverbs 6:30). The Year of Jubilee is also an interesting concept that gave grace and mercy and eased the penalty for some (Leviticus 27:24).

In the New Testament the classic example of restitution is that of the tax collector Zaccheus (Luke 19:8). Zaccheus, a tax collector appointed by the Roman Empire, was a shrewd operator and, besides keeping his Roman masters satisfied, squeezed out something extra for himself. Because of the protection he had from the Romans, Zaccheus' exacting of extra taxes for his own pocket could not be challenged, but he was despised and hated in his community.

Then he was confronted by the Lord Jesus Christ. He experienced a dramatic change of heart and attitude. His immediate response was to pay back those people whom he had cheated. Not only that, but four times what he had stolen from them! Zaccheus was not afraid to pay the price for his wrong-doing. He was prepared to confess it publicly and face the consequences. He obviously also had the financial means to make amends, and was willing to do so.

Even if we did not have such a well-documented example of restitution, the Christian moral and social ethic should produce compensation because love always seeks the best for others. It is obvious that a heartfelt confession, repentance and forgiveness should produce a desire to make restitution.

In the context of the South African situation, where so much human damage and schism has been suffered, there is a desperate need for true reconciliation among its many people and races. For reconciliation to have real substance, restitution should be made whenever possible.

However, tough questions still need to be answered:

❏ What kind of restitution needs to be made in each case? What is the cost of a human life?

❏ What if a guilty person will not or cannot make restitution?

Another matter which is being tackled by the new South African government is the restoration of land. Over the years, thousands of non-white South Africans were uprooted from their land and homes. There was mass resettlement. Today there is a clamour for restitution.

❏ How much do you pay a family that lost its home or land 15 or 25 years ago? In most cases it is impossible to restore the previous property. Do you pay market-related prices and, if so, would that be a satisfactory figure?

❏ Who decides if the restitution offered is fair?

❏ What happens when restitution cannot be made – for example, where families and relatives are deceased?

How it will all turn out will be a matter for history to decide. But in matters such as confession, forgiveness, restitution and mercy, there is no better institute to be involved than the church. It would be unfortunate if the issue was left solely to the legal minds of the country. If South Africa's Truth and Reconciliation Commission is to play a significant role in healing the nation, it must not omit the capacity of the church to bind the wounds.

13 UNHOLY ALLIANCES?

The issue of alliances with other religions caused some controversy among evangelical Christians in South Africa in recent times, when Christian leaders shared a public platform with leaders of other faiths.

Ray McCauley came under fire for accepting an invitation to serve on the Panel of Religious Leaders for Electoral Justice which was formed as an advisory organisation to oversee the country's first democratic election in April 1994.

Some Christians were shocked and appalled – more so when immediately prior to the election, Ray participated in a lunch-time prayer service for a peaceful outcome. Ray was seen on national television together with other Christian leaders, and Jewish, Muslim, Hindu and Buddhist representatives.

There was an outcry from several fundamentalist quarters, accusing Ray of compromising the gospel by taking part in the meeting. Some Christians have cautiously resigned themselves to this occasional occurrence, but still feel uneasy. Others have willingly and knowingly forged links with leaders of other religions.

Is this an issue which can been be judged wrong, as some fundamentalist Christians expound? The often used scripture is 2 Corinthians 6:14–15, which says:

'Do not be unequally yoked together with unbelievers. For what fellowship has righteousness with lawlessness? And what communion has light with darkness? And what accord has Christ with Belial? Or what part has a believer with an unbeliever?'

These verses are most often used when a Christian begins flirting with the idea of marrying a non-Christian, or when a Christian has an unsaved business partner. These verses are now being used by Christians who are wary of forming alliances with people of other religions. But what did Paul have in mind when writing these verses?

The term 'yoked' has a strong military meaning and alludes to a person leaving one army to join another – in other words, a switching of loyalties. The words 'fellowship' and 'communion' also indicate close and intimate relationships. When Christians decide to form an alliance with people of other faiths, there is neither a switching of allegiances nor intimate fellowship. Alliances, or common fronts, are formed on a limited basis. An alliance with Muslims and Jews on the abortion issue would in no way mean that Christians were forsaking their personal belief in Christ.

Christians deal with non-believers or people of other religions every day of their lives. If your bank manager is a Buddhist, does that mean you do not do business with him and his bank? What about the mechanic who fixes your car? What about the person who styles your hair? Or the person who serves you in the supermarket?

Christians do business with people of other faiths. Does this mean that your Christian faith is compromised? Are you tarnished by talking to and meeting with unbelievers? Certainly not. These are temporary business deals, not close, intimate fellowships. There is no switching of loyalty or betrayal of one's faith. Why all the fuss about Christians forming alliances with other religious leaders to combat moral decay in our country? Or in the case of the election, to ensure that fairplay prevailed?

Jonathan Edwards (1703–58), one of America's renowned evangelical theologians and revivalist, had strong views on Christians joining forces with non-Christians. He advocated that Christians should not hesitate to form a common front with others when threatened by a common foe. He demonstrated this when he supported the Massachusetts colony's decision to fight the French because of the threat to religious and political liberties.

Edwards argued that Christians have much in common with non-Christians – the same basic sense of good and evil – since God has etched his moral law on every human conscience. In fact, Edwards's public theology, keeping in mind his zeal as a revivalist, would not be popular with many fundamental Christians today.

In a nutshell, Edwards's belief did not call for Christians to create new and separate political communities beyond the church. He encouraged Christians to work with like-minded citizens, believers or not, to transform existing communities, according to the God-given principles of conscience.

He may have been a preacher who never minced his words when it came to God's judgement, but he was fully in favour of Christians playing a rightful and prominent role in public affairs, even if it meant forming alliances with people of other faiths.

The challenge to the Pentecostal, charismatic and evangelical church in South Africa is to roll up its sleeves and get involved in social action. In the past, much of this constituency has left this responsibility to secular society and sadly, many Pentecostals still adopt this isolationist view. They choose not to join with those outside the church as partners in common work for the community, but remain separated from society in an alternative community and as distant witnesses to the rest of the culture.

A better approach, and the one which is being adopted by some Pentecostals today, is to seek to transform culture from within – to be exactly what the Lord Jesus Christ urged His followers to be: light in places of darkness. Not just a distant lighthouse that flashes an occasional warning light. Christ's followers should always be on the cutting edge of society – in politics, the media, the arts, sport and business.

To achieve a better society means involvement, and it sometimes means forming alliances based on shared values and goals.

The famous British theologian, John Stott had this to say on Christian associations with other religions:

'Christians should indeed be in the forefront of those who are seeking global harmony. By God's creation we are one people in the world. We should be committed to international peace-making, participatory democracy, human rights, community relations, environmental responsibility and the search for a new international economic order.

'Moreover, people of different races and religions can, should and do cooperate in these kinds of social witness and action. In order to do so, however, it is not necessary to renounce our belief in the uniqueness of Jesus Christ. It would be folly to seek unity at the expense of truth, or reconciliation without Christ the mediator.'

14 Blood on the Streets

The ANC-dominated government has had some grand political achievements in its short rule since 1994. It has tried sincerely to allay the fears of many white South Africans by offering the olive branch of peace and reconciliation. There have been some outstanding examples of political cooperation between blacks and whites, at all levels, to uplift and reconstruct the nation.

Unfortunately, one glaring stain that is spreading through the nation and causing severe strain, and even panic, is the overwhelming wave of crime.

During the build-up to the national election there were serious incidents of crime and violence. Most people, including politicians, naively believed that the crime would abate once the euphoria of a newfound democracy swept the land. They were wrong. South Africa, sadly, has become the most violent country (outside of a declared war zone) in the world. Johannesburg, the commercial heartbeat of the nation, is the crime capital of the world. Tourists in downtown Johannesburg are often escorted by armed bodyguards during sightseeing walks in the city.

A senior police commissioner summarised the situation in the city by sketching the following scenario:

> 'Two men hold up a bank, grab the cash and run outside. But as they reach the curb they are mugged by two other thugs. These thugs grab the money, steal the getaway car and drive off. As they turn the corner they are hijacked and shot, and two other thieves make their escape!'

At cocktail parties in the wealthy suburbs of Johannesburg, the centre of attraction is the person who has *not* been mugged, burgled or hijacked. One member of Ray McCauley's church, Philip French, has been hijacked four times and shot twice!

Every day the newspapers are full of muggings, murder and mayhem. The streets of South African are becoming killing zones.

Suburban whites are building higher walls and homes that resemble prisons, with burglar bars on all windows, alarm systems and floodlights. A fortress mentality prevails and whites are increasingly quitting the country or preparing to leave. Unfortunately, these horrendous levels of crime aggravate racial tension and damage reconciliation efforts.

Many whites deride the government as weak-willed. Blacks, who are just as much victims of crime and violence, are diffident to come out strongly against the government.

The police chiefs cry out for more money, more staff and more support for 'get tough' tactics from the government. Sadly, the spiral of violence continues to sweep through the country. Statistics provided by the South African Police Services indicate that: one serious crime is committed every 17 seconds in South Africa; a housebreaking happens every two minutes; a robbery every five minutes; a murder every 30 minutes; and a rape every 18 minutes.

An amazing report appeared in a morning newspaper in Johannesburg which quoted the Lebanese ambassador saying it was safer to live in war-torn Beirut than to live in South Africa. He and his staff had suffered two attacks by armed thugs.

It was against this backdrop that Ray became increasingly angry and frustrated towards the end of 1995. It seemed that the government was unwilling to take stringent measures and that the police were, in fact, being overrun by the criminals. It was decided to launch a nationwide Stop Crime Campaign, a simple attempt to mobilise the public and to give them an opportunity to voice their frustrations about inadequate crime prevention strategies.

The nationwide strategy began with a top-level luncheon at the World Trade Centre near Johannesburg. Religious leaders, police chiefs and business executives were invited and, of course, the media. Ray briefed the meeting on the proposals and was enthusiastically supported.

This was the green light for him to initiate further luncheons across the country, targeting the major cities of the nine provinces. The ultimate goal was to mobilise the nation to observe a minute's silence at noon on 29 November.

One of the country's top radio stations, Radio 702, came out boldly to support the project. The police services were also eager. However, when push came to shove and businessmen were expected to put their money where their mouths were and donate funds for advertising, there was a sudden reluctance to get involved.

One prominent insurance company, which admitted paying out tens of thousands of rands in theft and car hijacking claims, ignored Ray's appeal for financial aid. They fobbed him off with the fact that they had donated toys with anti-crime slogans to children in Soweto.

The hesitation of business to commit wholeheartedly to the project was puzzling in view of an earlier pledge to government to fight crime and fund efforts to combat it. This strange reaction is highlighted by a telephone call I received from a former chief executive of a bank who said that the church should rather pray and not poke its nose into such affairs!

Despite this disappointment, there were businessmen who were willing to come to the party, notably Terry Rosenberg who, with Pastor Eric Tocknell, made sure that the city of Durban was solidly behind the project.

Another area of disappointment was the church and their congregations in general. From Ray's own experience he knew that there was hardly a church that did not have a member who had not suffered personally from the crime wave.

There also appeared to be hesitation from the government's side to show its full support for the campaign. We were to learn later that prominent government officials were wary of such a dramatic anti-crime campaign because they felt it would scare off international investors and give the country a bad name.

They need not have worried on that score. The international media were having a field day reporting countless crimes, including the theft of a cabinet member's limousine!

However, as the big 'standstill' day drew near, the Gauteng premier, Tokyo Sexwale, confirmed that he would attend the rally scheduled in the centre of Johannesburg. President Nelson Mandela agreed to send a message to be read by Ray at the rally. Other centres around the country arranged for similar rallies and marches to focal points to observe a minute's silence.

Members of the public were encouraged to wear a black ribbon and to tie a similar ribbon on their motor car aerials to signify not only a solemn remembrance of the victims of crime, but also to signify the 'death of crime'.

November 29 produced a mixed reception. Rain threatened for a while in Johannesburg. In Cape Town, rain and high winds ruined the event, but a hardy group of campaigners handed over a memorandum to the premier's office.

This memorandum, called 'The People's Memorandum', was drawn up in consultation with many people and given to the premiers throughout the country.

One of the nation's famous radio personalties, John Berks, brought a hushed silence to large parts of the nation at noon.

In many cities and towns, the public took the initiative and held hands in shopping malls, and in some places formed human chains across streets and roads, halting traffic for a brief moment.

The memorandum expressed the heartbeat of the ordinary person in the street. In part it read:

'We, the peace-loving and law-abiding people of South Africa express today our anger and frustration at the totally unacceptable level of crime and violence which is ripping out the heart of our fledgling democracy.

'The masses of South Africa have come through many years of oppression and deprivation. The cost of South Africa's new rainbow democracy has been paid for in blood and tears.

'Today we say to government do not allow this precious freedom to be stolen from our nation by villains and killers who threaten to turn our land into a jungle of crime and anarchy. We demand that the Government of National Unity and all nine provincial governments acknowledge, unequivocally, that we do have a major crisis, regarding crime and violence.

'In recognising that the nation is facing a national crisis we demand drastic and urgent action from the State and provincial governments.

'While recognising that many of the roots of the crime we are experiencing are the result of the dark political and social history of the country, we cannot allow this to be an excuse for an emphasis only on long-term solutions, while the majority of South Africans are subjected to a daily reign of terror.

'We want short-term to medium-term, decisive measures to be implemented now.

'The message to our government is clear and simple: act now and act tough on all criminals.

'The message from all good people to the criminals is also clear and simple: you will be exposed and hunted down. Crime will not pay.

'To this end the respectable and peace-loving people of South Africa solemnly pledge to refuse to participate in any form of criminality and to help the police and the government in all efforts to combat crime.

'We mark this day of 29 November 1995, as the beginning of a new, strong moral quality that will bind us together to make South Africa a place where we and our children can live in peace, safety and security.'

The memorandum included a number of demands and practical actions, many of which have since been implemented by the police. Despite continuing low-morale and shortages, the police have tried to stem the flood of crime.

Since this event, the police chiefs have asked Ray to help mobilise the religious communities to form a partnership to fight crime.

Adding to the police's frustration has been the highly publicised events of the Truth and Reconciliation Commission.

Victims of serious human-rights abuse have been allowed to give testimony, which has been broadcast on national television. Although we recognise the need to deal with the injustices of the past, it has rubbed raw nerves among many who still find it difficult to accept the police as their protectors and not as oppressors.

Much of the crime and violence is very public, but just as worrying is white-collar crime and an ominous increase in drug trafficking in South Africa.

The city of Johannesburg has become a magnet for thousands of illegal immigrants and businessmen from other parts of Africa. Large numbers of Mozambicans, Zaireans, Nigerians and Rwandese have arrived. Some are genuine refugees. Thousands are deported each month to Mozambique, but as they are unloaded from the repatriation trains, they begin the trek back to the cities of South Africa. These illegals are easy prey for employment in criminal activities or simply resort to lives of crime to survive.

Just as perturbing are the slick business operatives from West Africa who, the police say, are a main conduit for a massive drug trade into southern Africa.

These criminal elements offer a great challenge to the church, not only to stand against crime and violence, but to ensure that the next generation is given a platform built on sound morals and good values.

PART THREE
EVANGELISTICALLY POTENT

15 CHANGING LIVES

Adapted from a sermon by Ray McCauley

A recent survey conducted by the Coral Ridge Presbyterian church in the United States produced some startling information about the impact of evangelism in that country. The survey estimated that 25 to 33 per cent of all Americans claim a 'born again' experience. But what the survey also discovered was that 95 per cent of those Christians have never led another person to faith in Christ.

I find that figure shocking, but another statistic emerged that was just as startling. It estimated that 90 per cent of all new conversions in America resulted from the efforts of only three per cent of the churches in America.

Those figures should make all Christians sit up and take notice. If so much can be achieved by so few, imagine what the church could accomplish if it could mobilise its forces in a more effective soul-winning campaign.

To maintain its evangelistic potency, a church must always have compassion for people. The church must never become a country club. A church needs to desire to be a river of living water; if it does not do that it becomes a swamp.

Many of our Pentecostal and charismatic churches are simply stereotyped as 'happy-clappy centres'. There is also a tendency for many Christians to church hop, looking for the best 'dainties' available in town. There is often a lack of commitment to the local assembly.

The church needs to be a dynamic force that reaches out and touches the lives of the ordinary person in the street, in the shopping malls, in big business, on the sports fields and in the arts and media.

It is a staggering reality that the majority of people will not come to church voluntarily. You have to go out and bring them in. You cannot expect to reach a nation, a city or your community unless you reach out to those nearest to you.

In 1 Timothy 1:15 we read:

'This is a faithful saying and worthy of all acceptance,
that Christ Jesus came into the world to save sinners.'

If we could save ourselves it would not have been necessary
for Jesus to come to earth to die on a cross. If you can find
your own way to God, through your own work and through
your own brainpower or your own strength, you would not
need God's spectacular plan of salvation.

Some people think that Jesus was just a fancy prophet, or
that Jesus was just a good preacher or that Jesus is just one
of many ways to reach God. But it was John the Baptist who
proclaimed:

'Behold! The Lamb of God who takes away the sin of
the world!' (John 1:29)

That is why Jesus came. He came primarily to rescue the
people who inhabit Earth. That is something every church
leader and church member must always remember.

The criticism often aimed at ministers who venture into the
socio-political stream is that they are in danger of diluting the
very essence of the gospel. It is vital that the church always
maintains a powerful and potent evangelistic outreach.

In Matthew 9:10–13 we read:

'And so it was, as Jesus sat at the table in the house,
that behold, many tax collectors and sinners came and
sat down with Him and His disciples. And when the
Pharisees saw it, they said to His disciples, "Why does
your Teacher eat with tax collectors and sinners?" But
when Jesus heard that, He said to them, "Those who
are well have no need of a physician, but those who are
sick. But go and learn what this means: 'I desire mercy
and not sacrifice.' For I did not come to call the righteous, but sinners to repentance."'

Jesus, during His ministry, never isolated Himself. It may sound nice to be alone in a monastery, and to wait for the coming of the Lord, but it's not scriptural for Christians to isolate themselves.

God wants Christians to be among sinners. God wants you to be among worldly people. God wants you to walk boldly along the highways and the by-ways. God wants you to be where the action is, but God doesn't want you to be like them.

Christians are called to separation not isolation. Unfortunately, there are some Christians who haven't bumped into a sinner, except by mistake, in the last ten years!

There is a risk that Christians become so secure in their church building, enjoying the praise and worship, and the tongues and interpretation, that the hustle and bustle of the outside world passes them by.

It is certainly good for Christians to have security and a good church with a sound spiritual programme, but it has to be more than that. It was Charles Haddon Spurgeon who said that he would rather build a church at the gates of hell than have a cathedral in the best suburb.

The church is indeed a sanctuary, but it is more than that. I would like to think of it as, firstly, a hospital emergency centre where critically ill and injured people are taken.

No doubt some will censure you for getting out among sinners. Look what they said about Jesus:

> "'Why does your Teacher eat with tax collectors and sinners?" But when Jesus heard that, He said to them, "Those who are well have no need of a physician, but those who are sick. But go and learn what this means: 'I desire mercy and not sacrifice.'"'

Mercy is mixed with compassion and it compels people to see others as valuable and precious. So-called religious people may find it easier to make a sacrifice which makes them feel good than do the will of God.

There are people who think they can go to heaven by crawling up some steps on their bare knees, or through some other bizarre act of penitence, while the simple, biblical injunction is to love your next-door neighbour ... and your relatives that don't like you!

An experience that changed my life happened in Zimbabwe some years ago. A drunk person fell on the floor while I was walking to the elevator at the hotel where I was staying. His companions, who were also under the influence, tried to pick him up.

I looked at the scene with disgust and thought it was a disgrace. How useless they are. When I reached the lift and pressed the button, the Spirit of God pierced my heart and said, 'Son, the only difference between these people and you is Me.'

Jesus never came to call the righteous, but sinners to repentance. It is amazing when you see people behave as you used to behave. Christians sometimes forget where they came from. Coming to church with Bibles under their arms and looking so holy in the pews, it somehow slips their memory how they used to behave before they met Christ. Examine yourself, because true spiritual maturity doesn't breed arrogance, it breeds humility.

Proverbs 11:30 states:

'The fruit of the righteous is a tree of life,
And he who wins souls is wise.'

There has to be fruit in your church. There must be new blood coming into your church; precious people being saved and washed in the blood and brought to a new life in Christ.

Too often the church is simply playing a form of musical chairs and swopping address lists. The only newcomers you get are dissidents and rebels!

I mention the following statistics from our own church experience, not to brag, but to encourage and exhort, and to give God the glory. During 1994 in the Rhema Church in Randburg we had 1 600 children born again in our children's church. In all departments of the church we had almost 7 000 first-time decisions.

Now I am not boasting. Those are the results of preaching a potent gospel, not just from the pulpit, but in the streets and schools, and one-on-one witnessing.

Romans 1:16 states:

'For I am not ashamed of the gospel of Christ, for it is the power of God to salvation for everyone who believes.'

When you are enjoying reaping the harvest, never take it for granted. Don't ever think that is just some minor by-product of the church's programme. That would be a fatal error. Christians must never lose their compassion for people. It is the centre of the gospel because Jesus is the cornerstone of all that the church teaches and preaches.

The preaching of salvation and the gathering of souls is never an afterthought. We need to care and we need to see people as God sees them. Jesus said:

'What is a man profited if he gains the whole world, and loses his own soul?' (Matthew 16:26)

Some years ago Rhema, in cooperation with some other churches and organisations, formed an organisation called Christian Television (CTV) which was able to get airtime on the national television station on Sunday mornings.

The Rhema Church had an hour-long programme from 7.00 am to 8.00 am. To many people those early Sunday morning times may not look encouraging, but God has blessed the programmes to such a degree that up to two-million people watch them during the course of a month.

The church had telephone counsellors reporting for duty and they sometimes worked for two or three hours, dealing with response calls to our programmes. Besides dealing with hurting people and praying for special needs, dozens of people called in wanting to make a first-time decision for Christ. It became an exciting and rewarding outreach. Unfortunately, the programme was axed in February 1996, as part of the restructuring of religious services. We have protested strongly against what we have seen as unfair treatment of Christians.

However, one important thing the Rhema Church has learnt over the years is that there is no set pattern for saving people. Although we may have lost some of our potential soul-winning opportunities through television, it simply means that we must look for other openings to spread the Word.

For variety we once had a high-profile sports-stars' award event in which some of South Africa's famous past and present champions were invited to participate. There were also media personalities present. A sports commentator put up his hand very furtively when I gave the altar call and quickly put it down again. When I asked those who had raised their hands to get out of their seats and come to the front of the church, he remained seated.

I didn't make a fuss. I knew that God was dealing with the person. Later he came up to me and asked if he could see me privately. I took him to my office and prayed with him. I saw him a couple of weeks later at a big sports match. He waved and came to tell me that his life had been totally changed since he had prayed in my office.

Nicodemus came to Jesus by night. We don't mind how people come to Christ, en masse or one by one – as long as they come to accept God's gift of eternal life!

Not all people have the same experience and one needs to guard against prescribed formulas when leading people to Christ. Some weep real tears of sorrow in response to an altar call. Others walk straight out with no tears, no goose flesh, no Holy Ghost manifestation whatsoever. One sometimes wonders whether they are just coming out of curiosity to see what goes on at an altar call. But they say the sinner's prayer and ten years later they are as straight as an arrow for the Lord. There are some that have a Holy Ghost fit, fall over, scream, shout, jump and they're still going strong ... perhaps not hopping quite so high as the years go by!

In John 3:2–3 we read:

'This man came to Jesus by night and said to Him,

"Rabbi, we know that You are a teacher come from God; for no one can do these signs that You do unless God is with him." Jesus answered and said to him, "Most assuredly, I say to you, unless one is born again, he cannot see the kingdom of God."'

It is very difficult for people to perceive what the kingdom of God is all about until they have encountered the head of that kingdom.

Nicodemus said to Jesus, 'How can a man be born again?'

Nicodemus had no spiritual perception. You will encounter this often when dealing with people.

A reporter once asked me to explain to him 'this thing about tongues'. I did my best to explain it to him and then he asked me to speak in tongues so that he could write it down. He just had no clue about what I was trying to tell him. His mind was blind to the spiritual message. If that happens when you are trying to lead someone to Christ, don't get angry. Jesus had to deal with a learned man like Nicodemus, but He didn't turn around and call him an idiot.

'Nicodemus said to Him, "How can a man be born when he is old? Can he enter a second time into his mother's womb and be born?" Jesus answered, "Most assuredly, I say to you, unless one is born of water and the Spirit, he cannot enter the kingdom of God. That which is born of the flesh [the first birth] is flesh, and that which is born of the Spirit is spirit. Do not marvel that I said to you, 'You must be born again.'"' (John 3:4–7)

You can take a racehorse and a mule, and you can make the mule look beautiful. You can clean it and groom it every day, feed it the same food given to racehorses – in fact, you could turn it out to look as shiny as a thoroughbred. But one thing is certain: when the horse and the mule meet at the starting-gate, it is soon obvious which one is the mule!

If a person is not born again, they remain exactly as they

are. They may sit in a church all their lives, yet never make the decision that could revolutionise their lives and get them born again.

Remember the old story of the caterpillar and the butterfly? The caterpillar watched the butterfly flit past the tree trunk, showing off its beautiful colours. The greyish-brown caterpillar bemoaned his fate. He looked so ugly and useless. He wished that he could become a butterfly. One day the butterfly came and sat next to the caterpillar and told him he, too, could become a beautiful butterfly – if he allowed the miracle of metamorphosis to take place.

As we all know, when this wonderful process of nature takes place, the ugly caterpillar becomes a beautiful, airborne butterfly. That is something like the mystery of the gospel and the new birth. When that miracle takes place in the heart of a human being, they begin to see life differently. All of a sudden they have compassion for the souls of their friends and loved ones. The most selfish people suddenly have time for others. How many people would voluntarily give up their Christmas day to visit and cheer up the sick and poor? Not too many. But when our congregation is challenged to visit hospitals on Christmas day, they respond magnificently.

That is why religion and ritual alone are not the answer to life's problems. They do not produce the miracle of a new birth. Christianity is based firstly on the new birth and a personal relationship that produces a changed lifestyle.

One of the great off-putting aspects of the church has been its hypocrisy. Many young people have been put off church because of the behaviour of their parents, who were supposedly good churchgoers. Unfortunately, their Christianity stopped at the church door on the way out! What happened for the rest of the week was a sham and their children saw nothing real about God in their parents' actions and deeds.

The good news is that there is a breed of Christian who believes in the new birth and does reflect a life that is being moulded to the pattern that God desires.

Jesus is not coming back for a bound, defeated, empty,

powerless, unloving, selfish church. No, Jesus is coming back for a glorious, powerful, anointed, loving and caring church. In fact, the Bible uses the romantic term 'bride' when referring to the church.

Sometimes people relate Jesus to the church and think that Jesus and the church are the same. They are not. People should see Jesus first, in you, and then desire to come to church. Jesus said the gates of hell would not prevail against His church. The gates of hell are there for the church to break down and to enforce Satan's defeat.

The church should be tired of people telling us what they are. We need to see what they are.

The Bible says don't tell them you're a witness, rather *be a witness*. Sticking stickers all over your car, or wandering through the office mumbling prayers all day is not what the world is looking for.

What is it, then, that turns people to Christ? When you were once a miserable, selfish person, had an ugly mouth, always criticised and never cared about others, and then all of a sudden you arrive at work one morning with a new vocabulary, a smile and a caring attitude, people will know you have had an encounter with Jesus.

In Mark 16:19–20 we read:

> 'So then, after the Lord had spoken to them, He was received up into heaven, and sat down at the right hand of God. And they went out and preached everywhere, the Lord working with them and confirming the word through the accompanying signs.'

Signs should follow the Christian, not Christians following the signs! God will always confirm His Word. What the church needs to do is to obey the Word.

That is done by carrying out Jesus' great commission which is to win people to Him, disciple and equip them, and to go out and be the gospel.

What is our problem?

God looks for you to do the desiring so that He can do the

producing. But some people look for the producing before
they have the desiring. Let me add, it is so easy to lose your
first love.

One of the most difficult things I fight against in the ministry is not to get to a point where I see people as numbers.
I have to see people as valuable and precious. I have to see
them as people for whom Christ shed His blood. It is so
important to protect and maintain your love for God and the
things that He loves.

Seldom does a person encounter God without someone
else being involved. Even the apostle Paul, as Saul of Tarsus,
heard Stephen preach. While Stephen was being stoned Paul
held his garments and heard the first Christian martyr's
sermon. When Paul encountered Christ on the road to
Damascus it wasn't the first time he had heard the gospel.
As he lay in the dust he said, 'Yes, Lord.' He knew immediately that this was Christ, the risen Messiah.

God has chosen to work through people and to reveal the
gospel through believers. He uses your lips, your hands, your
feet to bring the gospel to other people.

In Matthew 9:35 we read:

'And Jesus went about all the cities and villages, teaching in their synagogues, preaching the gospel of the
kingdom, and healing every sickness and every disease
among the people.'

Just a note of warning. I believe that God heals today, but it
is not the centrepiece of the gospel. If it becomes that in your
gospel preaching, your ministry is becoming unbalanced.

Many years ago some people left our congregation because
they said I was compromising the Word of God by telling people to go to a doctor. If you have strong faith, that is fine – for
you. But don't try to force that on someone else who may not
be such a giant of faith! I fervently believe that God heals
today. I preach it and will never stop praying for the sick. But
that is not all I preach or minister. I have to maintain a balance when preaching the gospel.

The Bible states that when Jesus saw the multitude, He was moved with compassion for them because they were weary and scattered like sheep, having no shepherd.

> 'Then He said to His disciples, "The harvest truly is plentiful, but the labourers are few. Therefore pray the Lord of the harvest to send out labourers into His harvest."' (Matthew 9:37–38)

The problem is not with the harvest for it is plentiful, according to God. We cannot argue with that. Just look around you, at your relatives, your work place. There are plenty of sinners everywhere. The problem lies with the labourers. We need the loving heart of God to go out and be a witness every day, not just on Sundays.

The Bible declares in Romans 1:16 that the gospel is the power of God unto salvation. It is a potent, life-changing message that should always be fresh on our lips.

16 DESTINED TO WIN

Adapted from a sermon by Ray McCauley

There is a lot of interest these days in people trying to get a glimpse of the future. Fortune tellers, horoscopes and tea leaves readings are being employed by people seeking direction in their lives.

People should be warned that using occult methods is expressly forbidden in the Bible, but the good news from God's Word is that you have a great future. There is a godly plan and a destiny for your life.

In Ephesians 2:10 in *The Amplified Bible* we read:

> 'For we are God's [own] handiwork (His workmanship) recreated in Christ Jesus, [born anew] that we may do those good works which God predestined (planned beforehand) for us, (taking paths which He prepared ahead of time) that we should walk in them – living the good life which He pre-arranged and made ready for us to live.'

To help us find and focus on our destiny, we need to settle some issues which are foundational to our walking successfully in God's best. It is of the utmost importance to realise that you are not a mistake or an accident of nature. Your birth did not happen because your mother forgot to take the pill! Your birth did not take God by surprise.

This simple fact is so important because there are thousands of Christians wandering aimlessly in life, hanging on and hoping that somehow they will survive and make it to heaven. Many people have little personal esteem because they see no worth in themselves and cannot conceive that their lives could be of any significance among the billions who inhabit planet Earth. That is a lie which is robbing thousands of people of a rich and fulfilling Christian life. Instead of making an impact for God, many people see little or no purpose in their lives and countless more have no plan for how they are going to get from the cradle to the grave. Life for so many is a listless, humdrum existence.

But God has planned the exact opposite! He has a detailed plan mapped out for your life. Once you find it and focus your prayers and energy on fulfilling God's will, life becomes an exciting and meaningful experience. You no longer merely exist; you begin to live the abundant life which Jesus spoke about in John 10:10. Finding your destiny in God produces life, and where there is life there is excitement. Life becomes an adventure with God.

In Jeremiah 1:4–5 we read:

'Then the word of the Lord came to me, saying:
"Before I formed you in the womb I knew you;
Before you were born I sanctified you;
And I ordained you a prophet to the nations."'

This scriptural example wonderfully illustrates God's infinite interest and concern in the finest detail of your birth and subsequent life on earth. Your birth is not a mistake. You are of great value to God and you were created to fit into God's awesome plan for this world. In fact, your birth is a sign that there is already something finished that you have to start!

Another basic truth to finding and focusing on our destiny is to realise that you were born to be redeemed. Scripture emphatically declares that God is not willing that any should perish, but that all should come to repentance.

When the Lord Jesus Christ went to the cross, He had you in mind. God's plan of salvation for you is no accident, no mistake. It is part of the divine web of God's destiny for you to complete during your journey through life.

Another truth regarding destiny is to realise that God never starts something unless it is finished in His own mind. In other words, God does not map out a plan for your life and then push it aside and leave it incomplete. God, because He is the Perfect Planner, perfects His strategies and finishes them. It is up to us to find that destiny and then to walk in it. Grasp this simple fact: you are not born to find an assignment. You are born because of an assignment that God has already prepared.

To illustrate this point let me recount some of my personal experiences from my walk with God. I have, by God's grace, founded one of the largest non-racial churches on the African continent. I pioneered the church in 1979 with just 13 people in a home in Johannesburg. Today, we have a congregation of nearly 20 000 people, a nationwide television ministry and a godly influence that touches even the leaders of South Africa.

As I have studied God and destiny, I have come to realise that the establishment of the Rhema Church in South Africa, its phenomenal growth and its influence at national and international levels, are not just mere chance. Not at all. No, before I was born, God in His infinite power and wisdom saw our church in South Africa and the impact it would have. He destined tens of thousands of people to be influenced by the gospel through our church. God destined our church and myself to touch the lives of the rich and the poor, the famous and the obscure.

My birth, my early life and my Bible training were all fashioned because of a divine assignment that I was to become the pastor of the Rhema Church in South Africa at a special moment in time and history. That is an awesome thought. Yet it is also a most comforting and encouraging thing to know that you are walking in God's divine destiny.

When you find and focus on your destiny, absolutely nothing can stop God fulfilling His plan and purpose through you. Yes, there are obstacles. There are problems and challenges, but the sure knowledge that you are following God's destiny gives you incredible confidence to face the future and to believe God. It is all a walk of faith, but there are divine signposts of encouragement and blessing along the way.

One of the issues we need to settle once and for all is that God's destiny is far better than any other destiny for your life. True success is to know God's will for your life and to fulfil it. A stark reality is that you will not be judged on what you have done for God, but what He called you to do. A sad reality is that many people never fulfil their godly destiny.

How can you find and focus on God's destiny for your life?

You need to recognise that your ticket to greatness in the kingdom of God is often through small things. The world, we know, likes to build on gifts and talents, but God builds on character. Some things may appear small and insignificant, but they are never unimportant in God's kingdom. In seeking to fulfil God's destiny for your life, you need to realise that God wants to build character and maturity into your life.

I was a South African bodybuilding champion and competed in the Mr Universe championships in London where I attained third place. I used this talent during my early Christian life among young people. I would visit schools and university campuses, strip to the waist and do some poses, and then give a short testimony.

During those days I was drawn to a poor, down-town area of Johannesburg which I visited once a week. I used to go to a local bakery and fetch all the day-old bread, collect old clothes and take it to a hall in Doornfontein. The people there were desperately poor. Prostitution and drug-taking were rampant.

I remember trying to preach in a dirty old building with children yelling and screaming, and half drunk beggars lounging against the walls. Sometimes the air was so thick with marijuana that I became light-headed!

I never realised it then, but God was putting me through some tests. He was building my character. I was learning the lesson of faithfulness in preaching the gospel to the poor and of caring for those less privileged than myself. I was learning the lesson of serving God and preaching the gospel for the sole purpose of pleasing God. Today, I may be termed a successful pastor in the eyes of the world, but I know where my roots are. I have learnt lessons in humility – and continue to learn them – and God is able to entrust me with more of the destiny that He has for my life and ministry.

It says in the book of Habakkuk 2:2–3:

'Then the Lord answered me and said:
"Write the vision
And make it plain on tablets,
That he may run who reads it.
For the vision is yet for an appointed time;
But at the end it will speak, and it will not lie.
Though it tarries, wait for it;
Because it will surely come,
It will not tarry."'

Your responsibility is to have a godly vision before you, one that is in line with God's Word, and then simply to be the person that God created and called you to be. That applies to your career, whether in business, sport, entertainment or as a housewife. Live by the Word and practise the Word and you will find that your life and your career will slot into God's destiny for you.

If you have wandered and feel hopelessly out of God's will, be quick to repent and be restored, and get back in line with God's plan for your life.

There really should be no place for depression or a feeling of hopelessness in a Christian's life. When hopelessness takes hold of a person, it produces despair.

A French philosopher once said that people who despair insult the future. We could go further and say that for a Christian to despair is to insult God. How can we not be full of hope and faith when we realise that our lives are in the hands of not only an all-powerful God, but a loving heavenly Father? To fulfil destiny requires a positive, bold and courageous outlook.

There is a story about a salesman who went to a village in the heart of Africa and sent back a report to his factory which stated: 'No hope of any sales here ... nobody wears shoes.'

A month later a second shoe salesman visited the same village and sent back an urgent message: 'Great opportunity to sell lots of shoes. Hardly anybody has shoes here.'

It is like David and Goliath. To some people their Goliath looks too big and overpowering, but to the shepherd boy

David, Goliath was so big he could hardly miss him with his slingshot.

Perhaps you have tried to lead a God-fearing life, but have met with failure. Perhaps in your mind that failure disqualifies you from ever having a successful Christian experience. Remember, that failure need not be fatal in God's eyes.

The Old Testament is filled with the moral failures of some of the great men of faith. In the New Testament, Peter, Thomas and many of the other disciples displayed weaknesses and failure. But it was not fatal because they decided to put the past behind them and carry on.

I read a story which I hope will encourage you to forget the past defeats and carry on with renewed hope to win new battles and live victoriously.

In the 1920s, a British expedition made several attempts on the yet unconquered Himalayan peak of Mount Everest. There were three expeditions, but all ended in failure, tragedy and loss of life. At a special banquet arranged to honour the brave climbers who had lost their lives trying to climb the world's highest mountain, a surviving colleague turned his back on the guests and faced a photograph of the towering, majestic Mount Everest, which hung on the wall.

Looking at the picture the man made a speech in honour of the men who had died on the mountain. In closing he said:

'You defeated us once, you defeat us twice and a third time, but we shall some day defeat you because you can't get any bigger ... but we can.'

In 1952 Mount Everest was conquered.

Never forget that God has destined you to win the race He has put you in. Jesus did not give us an impossible task when He called us to be the salt and the light. He did not call us to defeat, but to victory through faith in His power and ability to equip us to be what He wants us to be. Let's not be victims, but rather victors. Let's be Christians who are courageous, single-minded and relevant to what is happening around us.

Don't let the devil try to deceive you into thinking the situation is too complicated and that your contribution will make no difference. Believe that lie and the church *will* fail to make an impact on the community and the nation.

Stop being a spectator and join the winning the team. The Bible says we are 'more than a conqueror'. Start believing and acting like a conqueror!

PART FOUR
RENEWAL

17 A River or a Swamp?

Adapted from a sermon by Ray McCauley

'But you shall receive power when the Holy Spirit has come upon you; and you shall be witnesses to Me in Jerusalem, and in all Judea and Samaria, and to the end of the earth.' (Acts 1:8)

In Acts 2 we read how the waiting disciples were all filled with the Holy Spirit and that they began to speak in other tongues. The Bible tells us that many people who saw them that day thought they were drunk with alcohol, but they were actually under the influence of the Holy Spirit.

We read in Acts 4:31:

'And when they had prayed, the place where they were assembled together was shaken; and they were all filled with the Holy Spirit, and they spoke the word of God with boldness.'

From Acts 2 to Acts 4, only two chapters later, the Scriptures teach that although the disciples had experienced the baptism of the Holy Spirit, evident by speaking in other tongues, they needed another infilling. In other words, they needed continual infilling of the Holy Spirit or constant refreshing.

We receive the baptism of the Holy Spirit at a certain place and moment in our lives, but then we need a fresh touch, some fresh oil. We actually need refreshing and infilling continually to live a successful and victorious Christian life. We need the Spirit of God to rise within us continually.

2 Timothy 1:6 states:

'Therefore I remind you to stir up the gift of God which is in you.'

We need to consider this very carefully because God, it seems, requires that we are not just filled as a one-off experience. It is something that He wants us to do on a daily, weekly, monthly and yearly basis.

Revelation 3:15 indicates that something contrary to this happened to many people in the church at Laodicea. Once this was an alive, on fire church, but at the time of writing, something negative had happened to many members of the congregation:

> 'I know your works, that you are neither cold nor hot. I could wish you were cold or hot. So then, because you are lukewarm, and neither cold nor hot, I will spew you out of My mouth.'

When a Christian is on fire for God, and is full of and controlled by the Holy Spirit, they hate what God hates and love what God loves. God does not like lukewarmness. He likes lukewarm people, but He hates lukewarmness in Christians. God would prefer a Christian to be cold rather than lukewarm, because at least when a person is cold everybody knows it. You know it yourself and people around you know it.

When a person is lukewarm they can pretend and get away with it in front of other people, but you cannot fool God. Sometimes Christians do not even realise that they have gone from the fire to the smoke!

The point that needs to be made is that many people become dissatisfied with their Christian experience. It may not be because of sin or disobedience, but a rather a yearning of the heart to experience something deeper or to regain a freshness to their witness. Other Christians battle with personal sins and find it hard to submit to the Word of God. They hunger for a dramatic and divine intervention that will cause a breakthrough and victory in their lives.

The heart's desire for a special touch or refreshing from God may be very pure, but here is a danger. People start chasing after the latest charismatic sideshow and sometimes it is not the Spirit of God, but something hyped up in the flesh.

There is also a tendency for Christians to seek a special blessing and then run back to their church and become critical of the pastor and other members of the congregation because the same manifestation is not happening there.

Pastors and leaders need to realise that we are not competing, but rather helping to complete the work of Christ in each other. Realising this simple fact helps to remove the notion that if a person has not 'got it' they are missing something.

One thing is certain: only God knows the intimate desires and motivations of the hearts and minds of people. He also knows what is best for each of His saints.

Romans 15:13 states:

> 'Now may the God of hope fill you with all joy and peace in believing, that you may abound in hope by the power of the Holy Spirit.'

1 Thessalonians 1:6 says:

> 'And you became followers of us and of the Lord, having received the word in much affliction, with joy of the Holy Spirit.'

There is little doubt that most Christians desire to be filled and touched by God. Christians want God to fill them, but unfortunately there is often much confusion when a new 'wave' begins to manifest in the church.

The problem has never been with God manifesting Himself. It has been with the administration of what God wishes to do among His people.

God's move in churches around the world may be sovereign, but He wants His people and leaders in the church to use wisdom when it comes to the administration of any 'new' outpouring or moving of God's Spirit.

When God moves and things begin to happen, Christians are sometimes too gullible and accept everything that is happening as from God. When one tries to correct them, they become hurt or full of pride, and arrogantly think they are better Christians because they have received some special manifestation.

Beware, it is not always so.

Remember that Lucifer, worshipping in the midst of God's presence, rebelled. People do not understand that in the midst of a manifestation and a move of God, one can find carnality, people with pride, people with wrong motives, people with selfish and arrogant ideas, people who allow themselves to be deceived, and abuse and misuse the precious anointing and power of God.

This observation is based on a solid biblical example. Let us examine the experiences of the congregation in the church at Corinth.

The apostle Paul comes to a church that is being used by God. The power of God is unmistakably evident in the church. There are many and varied manifestations of the Spirit of God. From all outward appearances, this was a church that could honestly have put up a billboard reading: 'Come and see the miracle working power of God.'

Yet the apostle Paul had some hard words and a lot to say to this church. He had to correct, instruct and explain things about the working and moving of God's Spirit.

Please take note of this: just because the Corinthians had all the gifts of the Spirit functioning in their meetings, this did not make them a super spiritual and mature church!

We need to take off our religious glasses and read the letter to the Corinthians, in particular chapters 12–14, and discover how their experiences apply to the church today, at the end of the 20th century.

It is important to note that the word 'gifts' used in 1 Corinthians 12:1 was introduced by the translators. Checking back into the original Greek one finds a slightly different intention in the wording. A more literal reading, much closer to the original is:

> 'Now concerning spiritual *matters,* brethren, I do not want you to be ignorant.'

Significantly, God says He does not want the church to be ignorant about spiritual matters. And the reason for this is found in 1 Corinthians 14:40 where the Scripture states:

'Let all things be done decently and in order.'

It is also needful to stress that Paul was dealing with what we would call the 'corporate anointing' or moving of the Holy Spirit in a church or public meeting.

How you and the Spirit of God operate in your quiet times is often very different. I know that some things I have done while praising and worshipping God in my bedroom would have caused more confusion than anything else if I did them in public, especially if I were sitting next to someone who was not saved!

It is clear to me that although Paul dealt with disciplinary issues in his letter to the Corinthians in the context of chapters 12–14, he is dealing specifically with the manifestation of the Spirit and how it should be administered. He does so to clear the confusion which reigned.

In 1 Corinthians 12:8–11 we read:

'For the one is given the word of wisdom through the Spirit, to another the word of knowledge through the same Spirit, to another faith by the same Spirit, to another gifts of healings by the same Spirit, to another the working of miracles, to another prophecy, to another discerning of spirits, to another different kinds of tongues, to another the interpretation of tongues. But one and the same Spirit works all these things, distributing to each one individually as He wills.'

Please note that it is 'as He wills'.

One Sunday night while I was preaching the Spirit of God urged me say: 'Tell a person in this auditorium that they've stolen money and they must put it back.'

I didn't blurt it out immediately, but at the appropriate time I spoke forth. It always takes faith to speak out. Your mind sometimes tries to get in the way. Little did I know that someone had stolen R1 300 from a desk in the administrative offices of our church earlier in the week. On Monday morning the money was back in its rightful place.

The point I would like to make is that if I stood behind the pulpit and claimed God has given me the doctrine of showing who steals, and every Sunday all we have is a 'who steals' time, the services would end in disarray. No-one owns the Holy Ghost when it comes to Him moving through a person. We cannot force it.

When I was a child I remember that the milkman would come personally to deliver milk and dairy products to our home. We always called this person the milkman, but he did not make the milk. All he did was deliver it. When a person ministers under the anointing of God, they are simply the vehicle or channel for delivery.

We read further in 1 Corinthians 12:12–13:

'For as the body is one and has many members, but all the members of that one body, being many, are one body, so also is Christ. For by one Spirit we were all baptized into one body – whether Jews or Greeks ...'

That means, whether you are Egyptian, Lebanese, Afrikaans, Zulu, Sotho, Anglican, Baptist, Methodist, charismatic, covenant saints, Rhema Church, or whatever, Jesus sees only one body and it consists of individual people who have accepted Christ as their personal Saviour.

Paul's dealing with the Corinthian situation is not unfamiliar to churches today who become confused when there is a move of God's Spirit. Paul reprimanded them for their critical spirit, their arrogance, manipulation and for the abuse that entered their meetings.

The Corinthian church could have challenged Paul and told him they were experiencing the manifestation of God's Spirit. In fact, they were used more than any other church in the district. In fact, they didn't know another church that had so much power and manifestations of the Spirit!

I would like to paraphrase Paul's response in 1 Corinthians 12:14–17 to make my point:

> 'For in fact, the body is not one member but many. If evangelist Reinhard Bonnke should say because I am not Ray McCauley, am I not of the body? Is it therefore not of the body? And if Billy Graham should say because I am not a Jack Hayford, I am not of the body, is it therefore not of the body? If the whole body were just like Billy Graham, where would the pastors be? Where would the teachers be? You wouldn't find one.'

You see, each part of the ministry has need of the other. We need the evangelist to go out and reach the lost. But we need pastors and teachers to make sure that those converts grow and become effective witnesses for Christ. An evangelist cannot say he does not need a pastor, just as a pastor cannot say he does not need an evangelist. Remember, God has set each of them in the body, just as He pleased.

I cannot say to the people who are looking after the babies in the mothers' room I have no need of you, or I don't need any Sunday school teachers. Without the support system of other dedicated Christians, the church could not function. If all the babies were yelling and screaming, and the children were fidgeting while the sermon was being preached, the church services would be a nightmare. We all need each other and we all have a function because God wants things done decently and in order.

I am sure that everything in heaven is organised in the most precise and correct manner. I am positive there is no rudeness, arrogance or nonsense behaviour in heaven. The trouble in the church is that people place people on pedestals and exalt them higher than even God would.

When we stand before God one day we will all be judged on what God called us to do, not what we have done. If it pleased God to call someone into a private life of prayer and intercession and that person has been faithful and obedient to that calling, even though you never knew about it, their reward would be greater than some flashy preacher who went into the ministry for his own self-interest.

Paul continues in 1 Corinthians 12:22–26:

> 'No, much rather, those members of the body which seem to be weaker are necessary. And those members of the body which we think to be less honourable, on these we bestow greater honour; and our unpresentable parts have greater modesty, but our presentable parts have no need. But God composed the body, having given greater honour to that part which lacks it, that there should be no schism [division] in the body, but that the members should have the same care for one another. And if one member suffers, all the members suffer with it; or if one member is honoured, all the members rejoice with it.'

The scripture is clear: if one member suffers we all suffer. In reality, though, that is not always the case. When some Christians hear about the failure of a brother or sister or minister, they often seem glad. If a church down the road backslides or a church pastor in leadership falls into sin, it hurts the whole body. Similarly, of course, when one member is honoured we all share in that honour.

Being a leader in a church or denomination can be very demanding and often your motives are misunderstood or incorrectly perceived. People will sometimes think you are proud or trying to act as though you are better than someone else. But we need to respect the calling of God on a person's life. When God's blessing and anointing are on a person and they are being used, we should not become envious or jealous. Rather we should rejoice with them. The joy and acclaim they receive are due also to the least in the body of Christ. No-one can succeed without the help and support of the other members of the church.

God placed me where I am, not because of me, but in spite of me. If God wants to use me to minister to a president or a nation, do not be jealous.

Paul asks a pertinent question in 1 Corinthians 12:29:

'Are all apostles? Are all prophets? Are all teachers?
Are all workers of miracles?'

The answer is, of course, 'no'. God does not want us to be copy cats. He created us as individuals and He wants us to operate as such, using the special gifts and talents that He has blessed us with, no matter how wonderful or menial they may appear. We must not try to clone ministers. We cannot have 500 graduates from our Bible School trying to act like Ray McCauley.

What Paul is saying in chapters 12–14 is simply this: He does not want the Corinthian church to be ignorant about the working of the Spirit. Then he moves to the most important part and says you can have the anointing, you can experience all the joy, you can have all the faith, but without love you are nothing.

Someone once said to me: 'Many people desire the spiritual gifts so that they can be loved, instead of desiring to walk in the love of God, and then operate in spiritual gifts.'

Paul says in the opening verses of the famous chapter 13 of the Corinthian letter:

'Though I speak with the tongues of men and of angels, but have not love, I have become as sounding brass or a clanging cymbal. And though I have the gift of prophecy, and understand all mysteries and all knowledge, and though I have all faith, so that I could remove mountains, but have not love, I am nothing.'

This is a general warning not to become spiritually arrogant if you have experienced something from God, or if you are used in the ministry in a special way. Don't get puffed up. Don't become judgmental. Don't try to put pressure on others to make them feel guilty for not experiencing what you have experienced. I am not saying that you must not pray and desire to be used by God. I think the reading from *The*

Amplified Bible of 1 Corinthians 14:12 sums it up:

> 'So it is with yourselves; since you are so eager and
> ambitious to possess spiritual endowments and mani-
> festations of the (Holy) Spirit, [concentrate on] striving
> to excel and to abound [in them] in ways that will build
> up the church.'

We hear much about church growth programmes. There are
seminars and conferences held around the world on the subject. Many of them are good because they show a desire by
ministers and the church to expand. But a most exciting way
to build a church is when the congregation is touched in a
supernatural way by the Spirit of God. Programmes can be
good and do serve an important role in the church, but they
can never be a substitute for the manifest power of God.

You build up a congregation when the people come back to
the pastor and tell him how God has ministered into their
lives by the Holy Spirit. I'm not talking about a quick-fix
thrill of the moment, but something real and tangible which
is easily measured by the change and growth of individuals
and the congregation.

I seriously doubt that people are truly being touched by God
when they still have the same old bad habits and still do not
tithe, but are always going on about the wonderful service
and the great blessing they got out of it. Those are, sadly,
phoney experiences and just encourage the label of 'hypo-
crite'. When God moves upon a person, demonstrably or gently and quietly within their hearts, genuine fruit should be the
result. When people are truly touched and ministered to by
the Holy Spirit, it is a joy for them to respond to special
prayer meetings or to get involved with this outreach or that.

The famous revivalist, Charles Finney, said that when a person is on fire for God, people will watch them burn. In other
words, you will be a witness. And when people see a change
in you, and the love of God manifesting through you, they
will want to come to your church and experience the same
life-changing power of God.

Paul says in 1 Corinthians 13:3:

'And though I bestow all my goods to feed the poor, and though I give my body to be burned, but have not love, it profits me nothing.'

Let us consider the other side of the coin. We have examined what Paul termed 'spiritual matters', but Paul touched on the social matters of the day when he mentioned feeding the poor.

Some people think that because they feed the poor, they are spiritually more mature than others. They ignore the supernatural gifts and escape into the world of 'good works'. It may become a substitute for genuine spiritual growth and maturity.

Don't think that because you are involved in helping the underprivileged it makes you a spiritual hotshot and gives you the right to run down others. Love is patient, and love needs to flow on both sides of what God is doing or not doing. Love is kind, it is tender hearted – it is not arrogant, it is not rude and does not parade itself. Love hopes all things, endures all things, bears all things. Love never fails. We need to be constantly reminded of this royal truth.

In chapter 14, Paul addressed the issue of the administration of the manifestation of God's power. The church at Corinth was having difficulty with people who were always babbling in tongues. They thought they were being super spiritual; they probably saw themselves as real pillars in the church. There are obviously times and places for speaking in tongues, but it needs to be done decently and in order, especially in a public service.

From time to time I present a short inspirational message on national television in South Africa which is broadcast just before the early evening news. If I went on the air and all I did was speak to the nation in tongues for a couple of minutes, they would think I had gone mad. I would never be invited back! It might sound and look very spiritual to some people, but it would be confusing for most and God would get no glory from a mess like that. It is my responsibility to present a spiritual message that, with God's anointing, will be listened to by the people watching television.

Things have to be done in their right setting and context. For example, if a small group gets together in a home for a prayer meeting, there is nothing wrong within the context of that meeting for people to spend some moments praying in tongues. It helps to set the tone and mood for the meeting.

In 1 Corinthians 14:20 we read:

'Brethren, do not be children in understanding.'

When I hear about the extremes that happen in some Pentecostal circles I have to ask the question: When are we going to grow up? Why do we so often end up with a swamp? What God intends for His people is a river that flows with power, anointing and blessing. But because of nonsense and lack of good, mature leadership, the river becomes a swamp.

Someone once asked me: 'Do you think Pentecostals are going to heaven?'

I replied: 'Yes, if they don't run past it.'

Paul is exhorting the Christians at Corinth to grow up in their understanding. In a sense we are to be like children when it comes to faith and trust in God as our heavenly Father. But in a very real way, God wants us to grow up in our minds and in our understanding.

Just watch young children and you will soon see that much of their enthusiasm and energy comes from pure emotion and not mental understanding. Emotions are God-given and there is nothing wrong with experiencing feelings of joy and ecstasy when we enter God's presence. But we cannot live purely on emotions; we need to come down to earth and face the sometimes hard and harsh realities of life.

In 1 Corinthians 14:28–33 we read:

'But if there is no interpreter, let him keep silent in church, and let him speak to himself and to God. Let two or three prophets speak, and let the others judge. But if anything is revealed to another who sits by, let the first keep silent. For you can all prophesy one by one, that all may learn and all may be encouraged. And the spirits of the prophets are subject to the prophets. For God is not the author of confusion but of peace, as in all the churches of the saints.'

One of the disturbing things that happens in some churches, is that experiences begin to take precedence over the preaching of the Word. People have a 'good feeling' and want to repeat that same type of service week after week. They are what I would term 'spiritual junkies'.

If the Holy Ghost speaks through the minister as he preaches the message, surely the Holy Ghost is not confused by interruption when someone jumps up and wants to bring a tongue or prophecy?

If, during a service, a person feels a strong anointing and an urge to bring forth something from the Lord, they have three choices. Firstly, if it is clearly a corporate anointing, the pastor will, or should, have the spiritual perception and common sense to be quiet and let the Lord move in the meeting.

This happened from time to time in our church. One Sunday morning the Spirit of God told me to sit down and keep my mouth shut. The Spirit of God began to move and I saw people lying prostrate before God while others wept or were touched in different ways by God.

Secondly, if people cannot contain themselves, they must leave the auditorium. In our church, we have sometimes escorted people out. God wants decency and order and no confusion. What He wants is sound and wise administration. People need to be taught these things.

Thirdly, the person can control themselves and submit what they believe they have received from the Lord to the leadership of the church. That is the way it is done in my church. If anyone thinks they have a word from the Lord, they come quietly to the pastoral section of the auditorium and tell one of our leadership what they believe the Lord has laid on their hearts.

The leader will either give the person a green light and I

will call him or her forward to share it with the rest of the congregation. This is done quietly and respectfully without disrupting the whole meeting. If they don't get a green light, they quietly return to their seats. The congregation appreciates what we are trying to do and no-one is offended. Sometimes the timing of the word may be inappropriate and that is why we need to judge it first before it is exposed to the whole congregation.

I emphasise this is administration – not control. Our church is always open to the moving of God's Spirit and when He wants me out of the way, I gladly move over.

In 1 Corinthians 14:37–38 we read:

> 'If anyone thinks himself to be a prophet or spiritual, let him acknowledge that the things which I write to you are the commandments of the Lord. But if anyone is ignorant, let him be ignorant.'

My heart is committed to seeing genuine miracles and genuine healings. My heart is committed to seeing the church move with integrity and transparency. The church needs to be real. Sadly, there has been too much hype, abuse and manipulation in the church over the years.

Pentecostals and charismatics, because of their distaste for religious ceremony, often go to the other extreme as if they are trying to prove their spirituality. These people sometimes believe that when there is too much order in a meeting, God has not blessed the service!

There is no need for God's people to be ignorant of spiritual matters. God, I believe, wants to bless His people abundantly. He wants a river of blessing, anointing and power to flow through churches in every nation.

Let us not get in the way through childish ignorance. Let us be the fiery blessing that glows in every bit of darkness in this world.

18 THE FIRE

Adapted from a sermon by Ray McCauley

One of the things that disturbed me when I became a Christian was when I was told that God required something of me without explaining the reason. I believe the worst thing we can tell a child is not to do something and when they ask you why, you say, 'Because I said so'.

We are often like that with the Lord. We speak about the fire of God having fiery zeal, or someone who is on fire for God. The question is, what is the fire? Why the fire? Why do we need it? Why does God want it in our lives?

Luke 3:16 says:

> 'John answered, saying to them all, "I indeed baptize
> you with water; but One mightier than I is coming,
> whose sandal strap I am not worthy to loose. He will
> baptize you with the Holy Spirit and with fire."'

The holy fire of God is in your life so that you can fulfil your destiny. How many Christians do you know who get burnt out, discouraged and depressed because they are confronted with tests and trials? One thing is certain: the devil does not want any Christian, pastor or leader to fulfil their destiny in God. This is a threat to Satan's kingdom of darkness.

God, in His great redemption plan, has chosen to work through people to achieve His designs and purposes. Take note, though, that the devil works through people too!

You need to understand that God wants to use you – not only the pastor or the elder or the deacon. Each individual is created anew by God to fulfil a plan and a purpose. God wants you to succeed in reaching the destiny that is mapped out for you.

Often, as God works through people, others get in the way. It is like a dirty pipe with water running through it. The water is clean, but as it gushes through the pipe it collects dirt and dust and comes out muddy. That is the way it is with the human vessels God chooses to use. There is no perfect human vessel.

Why does God use Joe Bloggs when He knows through His divine foreknowledge that he is going to become a polluted channel? The reason is that God is always true to His own laws and principles. He wants to achieve something through you. When you stumble and fail, God does not throw you on the scrap heap. You may disappoint God, you may even disobey Him, but God's desire, plan and purpose remains the same. He wants you to become a strong, mature and obedient child to fulfil your life's mission on this earth.

Let me give you an example. You may say, 'I don't care what God wants for my life, I'm not going to give to that ministry, I'm not going to give any more because every time I've given, they've messed it up.'

Realise that God wants to use you to bless someone else. If you refuse to sow your money, time, energy or talents, God's sovereign principle of sowing and reaping is violated, not by Him, but by you. Who gets hurt?

It is like a farmer saying that he is tired of his farm, his workers and the weather and that he is not going to plant crops. When it is harvest time and the other farmers are reaping, the farmer asks where his harvest is.

God wants to operate and minister through you, not only to touch others, but also so that you can begin to operate in biblical principles.

Almost everyone wants to fulfil their destiny. But, let us be frank, I know that over the past 20 years in ministry, it has made me weary at times.

We need to have the fire burning in our lives – always. We need a fresh touch and anointing from God regularly. Then it becomes possible to complete our course in life.

2 Timothy 1:6–7 from *The Amplified Bible* reads:

> 'That is why I would remind you to stir up – rekindle the embers, fan the flame and keep burning – the [gracious] gift of God, [the inner fire] that is in you by means of

the laying on of my hands [with those of the elders at your ordination]. For God did not give us a spirit of timidity – of cowardice, of craven and cringing and fawning fear – but [He has given us a spirit] of power and of love and of calm and well-balanced mind and discipline and self-control.'

When you are filled with the Holy Ghost, one thing should be evident and that is that you will overcome any fleshly timidity. Have you ever watched people when they get drunk on alcohol? They lose their timidity and do wild, outrageous things. When a Christian is full of God's Spirit, they should be full of courage and boldness.

In Isaiah 9:7 we read:

'Of the increase of His government and peace
There will be no end,
Upon the throne of David and over His kingdom,
To order it and establish it with judgement
    and justice,
From that time forward, even forever.
The zeal of the Lord of hosts will perform this.'

We need zeal. I often say that it is better to be a wet water walker than a dry boat Christian. It is better to have a congregation full of zeal than one full of nothing. However, untamed zeal can be dangerous. The responsibility of church leadership is to channel the zeal so that God's purposes are fulfilled. Christians need fire and zeal to get results. One of the worst things in life is to be in the business of helping people but never appearing able to help them. How can we fulfil what God is calling us to do? How can we ever accomplish the vision for our churches, our communities and our nations?

Many Christians had visions and dreams, but many have become distant, faded memories. Some were once on fire for God, but have become tired and fallen out of the race.

In South Africa Christians, in particular, have faced many harsh changes in their lives over the last four to five years.

Political and social pressures never experienced before have tested even the strongest. As a result many have adopted a 'fort mentality'. They are now enduring; they are surviving, waiting hopefully for the return of the Lord.

That may sound reasonable and comforting, but I believe that God wants His people to achieve more than just survival. He wants His people to use their talents, their imaginations and to dream the big dreams which can only be fulfilled through God.

For some the fire has burnt very low. In fact, for some it is only a smouldering ember. They are more smoke than fire!

Jesus gave His followers fair warning about the road ahead. The Word says that tests and trials will come; there will be persecution and affliction. Jesus cautioned Christians about the cares of the world and lusts for other things. These are all realities of Christian life. We do not live in a monastery. We are not isolated from the world, but we need to learn how to overcome the world.

When you are on fire for God, life is not boring. The Bible states in Habakkuk 2:2–3:

> 'Write the vision
> And make it plain on tablets,
> That he may run who reads it.
> For the vision is yet for an appointed time.'

Have you shelved your vision because there is no enthusiasm in your walk with God?

The fire of God is a holy fire. It burns out all the rubbish in one's life. You begin to hate what God hates, and love what God loves.

Someone once said that when you get so busy doing the do's, you haven't got time for the don'ts. God loves righteousness and, when you are on fire for Him, you love His Word and desire to obey it.

Jeremiah 20:9 reads:

> 'Then I said, "I will not make mention of Him,

Nor speak anymore in His name."
But His word was in my heart like a burning fire,
Shut up in my bones;
I was weary of holding it back,
And I could not.'

The fire and the presence of God in Jeremiah's life were so intense that he could not help but proclaim the message. When you have the love of God burning in you, you love His Word and you behave differently.

We need to remember that the word 'Christian' did not originate in the church. It originated from non-believers who identified people who looked and acted like Jesus. They said: 'Here come the look-alikes, anointed ones. They do what their Master used to do. They get the same results as He did.'

You are not God, but an unbeliever needs to see God's love, humility and compassion in you. The fire is needed so that you can be a witness. The difference between Christianity and religion is simply that you are being something that is part of your nature. It is not a cloak or a mask that you wear at certain moments in your life. Being a witness is simply an extension of what you are.

Acts 1:8 states:

'But you shall receive power when the Holy Spirit has come upon you; and you shall be a witnesses to Me ... to the end of the earth.'

Being a soul winner does not necessarily make you a witness, but you cannot be a witness without being a soul winner.

That may answer some questions that trouble people. The gifts and callings of God are without repentance. When God calls a person and places them in a position of, say, an evangelist, it is a gift. That person did not earn it. It is simply a sovereign decision.

If that evangelist were to get involved in sin, the gift that God has given him to lead others to Christ does not disappear. He is still able to lead people to the Lord. Gifted ministers have come and gifted ministers will go. They may be recognised as great soul winners and operate successfully for a time, but eventually their life in God collapses inwardly, and their outward ministry will crumble. Unless that person repents, he or she will eventually be exposed.

Tragically, the recent history of the church is littered with ugly shipwrecks because ministers of the gospel have succumbed to temptation. But that is not an excuse for Christians not to seek God's highest goal for their own lives. When a Christian falls from grace it hurts us all, but it is no excuse for us to quit. The race is hard, but the rewards are eternal.

We need to strive to be witnesses wherever we go. The church building is not the focus of our evangelism, but an everyday place of work, study or play.

During the South African professional golf tour I give a Bible study for several South African and international stars. One of these is the well-known South African professional, Gavin Levinson.

One evening he came to tell me that his young son, Neil, had been to a specialist and was suffering from curvature of the spine. The doctor told him they would need to place special rods in his back and that he would not be able to play any sport. It was a rough time for the youngster. Gavin said that his son had asked that I pray for him because he believed God would heal him and that the doctors would confirm it.

Gavin asked me right there, in front of other golfers and sports personalities, if I would pray for his son. My first reaction was, what happens if this child is not healed? Then I thought, God knows this situation better than I do and God is not going to let a child become totally disillusioned, especially when he initiated the request.

If the father or I had said, 'Don't worry, God will heal you', that would have been different. But this child had placed himself in a position to receive from God. I agreed to pray for Neil and told everyone to gather round. Neil said he felt warmth throughout his body and felt 100 per cent better.

They returned to the doctor the following week. I wish Christians would learn from the manner in which the family approached the doctor. They did not barge in and say: 'God's healed my son, everything is fine, and you all need to be saved.' They simply asked the doctor to recheck Neil's condition before they made the final decision to carry out the proposed surgery.

They took another set of X-rays and when the doctor returned he said: 'I need to tell you that either I made the worst mistake last week, or something supernatural has occurred.' That was proof for Neil and his father and it is a powerful witness of real Christianity.

God helps us to be hungry to be on fire and anointed witnesses. Let's stop being self-centred and set the world alight for Jesus.

We need God to anoint us supernaturally to bring solutions to our churches, communities and nations. Solutions will not come from lukewarm and whimpish Christians.

We need to see the big picture and realise that our destiny is absolutely secure in God, because it is His will that we complete the tasks He has set for us. True success is to do what God wants us to do and to be faithful. That is why we need the fire of God.

If you have wandered and feel hopelessly out of God's will, repent and be restored, and get back in line with God's plan for your life. 1 John 1:9 states:

'If we confess our sins, He is faithful and just to forgive us our sins and to cleanse us from all unrighteousness'.

The blood of Jesus cleanses us of *all* sin – past, present and future. Paul's words to Timothy are recorded to encourage us:

'I have fought the good fight, I have finished the race, I have kept the faith. Finally, there is laid up for me the crown of righteousness, which the Lord, the righteous Judge, will give to me on that Day, and not to me only but also to all who have loved His appearing.'
(2 Timothy 4:7)